THINK SHARP

How Anyone Can Master Critical Thinking and Problem-Solving for Smarter Decisions and Career Success

Renae C. Linde

Contents

Why Thinking Sharper Matters Now

The Signal Beneath the Static

We used to say knowledge is power. Not anymore. Conflicting advice is constant. Half the solutions break more than they fix. We're flooded with options and starving for clarity.

Maybe you've felt it. That low hum of mental fatigue before lunch. That moment when a simple choice, what to prioritize, how to respond, whether to speak, feels heavier than it should. Not because you lack intelligence. But because you're saturated. Overstimulated. Distracted. And if you're honest, a little disoriented.

It's not your fault. But it is your problem.

In most work environments, what gets rewarded isn't nuance, it's speed. Certainty gets more traction than thoughtfulness, even when it's unearned. The loudest wins, even when it's wrong. The most confident opinion gets mistaken for the most credible one. In meetings. In media. In your own head.

That's why critical thinking isn't a luxury skill anymore, it's survival gear. It's the ability to pause before parroting. It means catching the moment before you react. Choosing sharper, even when the pressure's high.

This book isn't about becoming more knowledgeable. It's about becoming more clear. Clear about your values. Clear about your logic. Clear about the games people play, and the ones you unconsciously play with yourself. Because clarity isn't just a trait. It's a skill. And like any skill, it can be trained.

What's Broken Isn't You, It's the Way You've Been Taught to Think

Here's the ugly truth: most of us were never really taught to think. Not in school. Not at work. Not in the conversations that shaped us. We were taught to comply. To memorize. To produce. To argue or appease, depending on the context. But rarely to pause, examine, and refine our thinking before unleashing it.

And now? We're trying to make high-stakes decisions with low-quality thinking tools. We're trying to navigate conflict with communication habits we picked up in stress, not strategy. We're using default settings built for a slower world, and wondering why we're stuck.

Thinking isn't just about logic. It's about leverage. You can have all the right data and still make the wrong call if you haven't calibrated how you think. If you haven't trained yourself to detect bias, spot faulty logic, question assumptions, or separate clarity from charisma.

That's what this book gives you: the mechanics of sharper thought. Not theory. Not fluff. Just the skills that actually work when your brain is overloaded and your calendar is full.

Why This Book? Why Now?

I wrote this book for people like you. Smart, capable professionals who are tired of overthinking, tired of bad advice, and tired of watching poor decisions wreck projects, teams, and trust. You don't need inspiration. You need tools that hold up when things get loud.

If you've ever left a conversation thinking, "I wish I'd said that differently," or walked away from a decision feeling like your gut and your logic were at war, this book is for you. If you've ever felt pressured to agree with a bad idea because pushing back seemed too risky, you're not alone. And you're not powerless.

Think Sharp gives you an edge. Not by making you robotic. But by making you responsive. Intentionally. Strategically. With emotional realism and practical traction.

No jargon. No empty frameworks. Just straight talk, real tools, and case-based simulations that help you apply what you learn, so it doesn't evaporate under stress.

The Stakes Are Higher Than You Think

Here's what's at risk when your thinking isn't clear: time, trust, money, influence, and energy. Every day you spend in reactivity mode, putting out fires, second-guessing your choices, rewriting that email for the third time, you're draining resources you can't get back.

And when you're not thinking clearly, you don't just lose time. You lose traction. You defer hard conversations. You avoid smart risks. You let poor ideas dominate meetings because you didn't have the language, or confidence, to challenge them effectively.

Worse, you stop trusting your own judgment. You outsource your decisions to whatever sounds the most persuasive in the moment. You confuse charisma with competence. You chase "life hacks" instead of building durable skills. And one day, you look up and realize that you've been playing someone else's game with someone else's rules.

This isn't just about being smarter. It's about being less trapped. Less reactive to pressure. Less swayed by noise. Less likely to become the bottleneck in your own life.

Who This Book Is For

This book is for people who are intellectually curious but mentally tired. People who are good at what they do, but know they could be sharper, faster, calmer under pressure. People who feel the pressure to "show up" but aren't always sure how to show up with clarity when emotions are high or decisions are messy.

It's for anyone who's ever had to make a tough call without enough information. Anyone who's ever been cornered by a manipulative question or blindsided in a group conversation. Anyone who's ever wondered if they were being too sensitive, or not sensitive enough.

More specifically, this book is for:

- Professionals who need to communicate ideas persuasively.

- Managers who want to navigate disagreement without resorting to dominance or avoidance.

- Entrepreneurs, freelancers, and career changers who face high-velocity choices and can't afford to stall.

- People in transition, whether upscaling, pivoting, or recovering from burnout, who are rethinking how they think.

If you've ever said, "I just don't have the bandwidth for this," or "I know what I mean but I can't explain it," or "I wish I could figure out what's really going on in this situation", you're exactly where you need to be.

What Makes This Book Different

Think Sharp doesn't give you recycled TED Talk wisdom or generic personality frameworks. It doesn't pretend that "staying positive" is a thinking strategy. And it doesn't talk down to you with fluff disguised as clarity.

Instead, it gives you:

- Real frameworks for filtering noise, making decisions, and prioritizing what matters.

- Practical exercises that help you spot your own thinking traps, and sidestep them before they cost you.

- Emotional and psychological insight that respects the complexity of real-world choices.

- Tools for communicating ideas with more clarity, persuasion, and impact, especially under pressure.

- Strategies for balancing logic and emotion so your decisions are both smart and human.

You won't find any magic pills here. But you will find something better: This is more training ground than think tank, where clarity gets pressure-tested instead of polished.

How the Book Is Structured

This isn't a book you skim on a lazy Sunday and forget by Monday. It's designed for action, deliberate, thoughtful action that reshapes how you engage with your world. The structure follows a clear arc, starting with foundational skills and ending with advanced strategies for resilience and growth.

Each chapter builds on the one before it, with momentum and precision:

Part I: The Foundations

We begin by decluttering your mind. You'll learn how to manage information overload, detect biases and fallacies, and apply simple but powerful frameworks to decision-making. This section sharpens your mental filter.

Part II: Strategic Problem Solving

Now that you've cleared the fog, it's time to solve harder problems. We explore emotional intelligence, creativity, failure-proofing your decisions, and systems thinking, all in ways you can use at work, at home, or anywhere clarity is needed.

Part III: Communication Mastery

Good thinking means little if you can't express it. This section helps you present ideas persuasively, build arguments that resonate, and overcome the static that plagues most conversations. We'll tackle communication barriers, team politics, and emotional landmines head-on.

Part IV: Creativity on Demand

Problem-solving isn't always linear. This part introduces creative ideation tools and reframing techniques that stretch your thinking. You'll learn how to brainstorm with more purpose and less chaos, and how to break patterns that limit innovation.

Part V: Practice and Application

Real-world exercises. Interactive simulations. Reflective prompts. This isn't filler, it's where theory becomes practice. Whether you're trying to prep for a negotiation, work through a team conflict, or assess a recent mistake, this section gives you a safe place to train.

Part VI: Emotional Intelligence in Action

Here, we focus on team dynamics and personal growth through the lens of emotional clarity. Think: conflict resolution, empathy under pressure, and how to support others without losing your own boundaries.

Part VII: Navigating Real-World Challenges

We get tactical. You'll learn how to cut through workplace politics, manage fear of change, and break out of unproductive habits. We take the principles from earlier chapters and pressure-test them in high-stakes environments.

Part VIII: Sustained Growth

The final chapter is about staying sharp, keeping your momentum when the novelty wears off. We'll talk about tracking your growth, adapting to new challenges, and building habits that strengthen clarity over time.

You can move through the chapters linearly, or jump to the section that fits your current need. Either way, you'll find tools, not just ideas, strategies that respect your time and your intelligence.

Why You Can Trust This Process

This book wasn't written from a pedestal. It was written in the middle of real work, real conversations, real failures. I've coached aspiring leaders who couldn't articulate what they wanted until the moment had passed. I've worked with professionals who knew they were burned out but didn't know what to cut. I've been in rooms where the smartest person had no influence, and the most manipulative one ran the show.

These pages are built from lived experience and psychological research, tested under pressure and refined in mess, not in theory.

What most people need isn't another overhaul. It's a small shift that sticks, something quiet, practical, and lasting.

Before You Begin

One final word before we dive in: this isn't about thinking harder. It's about thinking better. That means slowing down when it counts. Speeding up where it helps. And learning to trust your mental process, not just your instincts or your spreadsheets.

You'll be tempted to skip the reflection questions. Don't. That's where the muscle gets built. You'll be tempted to nod at an insight and move on. Don't. Pause. Apply. Come back to it in the context of your own real, messy life.

Thinking sharp isn't about always having the right answer. It's about knowing why you believe what you believe. It's about making choices you don't second-guess later, not because you're infallible, but because you've learned to check your footing before you leap.

We don't rise to the level of our intentions. We fall to the quality of our thinking. And that quality isn't something you're born with. It's something you build.

Let's get to work.

1

Mastering the Foundations of Critical Thinking

The Art of Filtering Information Overload

If your brain feels like a browser with too many tabs open, some of them auto-playing video ads in the background, you're not imagining it. Information overload isn't a productivity buzzword. It's a cognitive liability.

We live in a world where information doesn't arrive quietly. It ambushes. Notifications, Slack pings, hot takes wrapped in newsletters. By the time you finish your second coffee, six voices have told you what to think.

In this environment, the problem isn't access. It's filtration. The most effective thinkers aren't the ones who know the most.

They've built systems that filter out the noise and protect their focus.

Why You Need a Filter, and Not Just a Stronger Will

Most people think they can simply try harder to stay focused. What they really need is fewer inputs and smarter boundaries. Your attention is finite. Your bandwidth isn't something to stretch, it's something to protect.

When every ping feels urgent, your brain stops noticing what actually matters. That's not just a time management problem. It's a cognitive overload problem. When your brain is constantly shifting between stimuli, it can't enter the mental state required for deep thinking. Instead, you stay in a loop of reaction. You stay efficient, but it's the kind that costs clarity.

Good decision-making starts upstream. Before you reflect, analyze, or act, you have to get ruthless about what you let in.

The Three-Layer Filter

Treat incoming data like a bouncer at capacity. If it's not on the list, it doesn't get in. You sort by relevance and risk.

Here's a basic three-layer filter that works in real time:

- Signal vs. Noise

Is this actually useful? Does it shift how I think or act? Or is it just loud? If it doesn't help you make a better decision, take a smarter risk, or strengthen your perspective, it's noise.

- Now, Later, or Never

Timing matters. Do I need this information today? Is it prep for something a week out? Or is it the kind of thing that feels useful but never actually gets used?

- Depth vs. Width

Are you going deeper into something that matters, or just grazing across headlines to feel informed? Wide information builds a sense of awareness. Deep information builds insight. You need both, but not at the same time.

Case Study: The Drowning Manager

Amanda was a senior project manager in a fast-scaling tech company. Her title was impressive. Her daily reality: chaos. She started every morning with good intentions and ended every day feeling underwater. Calendar stacked. Slack unread. Browser tabs in the triple digits.

Amanda blamed her calendar. But the overload started before her day did, with how much she was letting in. She was mistaking "staying informed" for "being prepared." Constant exposure was giving her stress, not clarity.

She rebuilt her information diet using the three-layer filter. She cut the noise, newsletters, Slack channels, dashboards, until what was left actually helped her think. Canceled a biweekly update call that didn't actually update anything. Then she reclassified her inputs:

- Direct-impact (project data, client changes)

- Strategic-trend (monthly digests only)

- Personal-growth (limited to one source per week)

The result? Her brain got quieter. Her meetings got sharper. She went from reactivity to authority, without working longer hours.

Tactical Filtering (That Actually Works)

It's easy to say "filter your inputs." Harder to do it when you're in the thick of things. These tactics work because they're grounded in behavior, not idealism.

- Triage in Real Time

Don't "come back to it later." Decide when it arrives. Use a five-action system: Trash, Archive, Delegate, Act, or Save to Read Later, with a tool, not your memory. Notion, Instapaper, Readwise, take your pick.

- The Daily Top 3

Pick three high-value input sources. That's it. If you want more, swap something out. Information hoarding isn't strategy. It's fear dressed up as diligence.

- The Weekly Cull

Once a week, purge your feeds. Unsubscribe. Mute. Unfollow. Set intentional limits. This isn't about minimalism. It's about cognitive autonomy.

- Track Your Switches

Tools like RescueTime will show you how often you bounce between tabs or apps. Spoiler: it's probably every 40 seconds. Awareness here isn't about guilt, it's about data. You can't fix what you don't see.

- Build a Second Brain

Tiago Forte's PARA model (Projects, Areas, Resources, Archive) is a good starting point. You're not just collecting data. You're building a retrievable system for action. It's not hoarding if it's organized, and used.

The Invisible Cost of Unfiltered Inputs

The real cost of information overload isn't lost time. It's cognitive drag. Every half-read article, unresolved notification, or vague mental to-do list becomes residue. You think you're ignoring it. But your brain is spending resources to keep ignoring it.

This is why decision fatigue shows up by lunch. Why simple choices feel harder than they should. Your RAM is maxed out.

Effective thinkers aren't more disciplined. They're more decisive about what deserves their attention in the first place.

Think of Filtering as a Thinking Skill

Filtering isn't just a time saver. It's a thinking enhancer. It makes space for what matters. It sharpens your judgment before you even sit down to make a decision. It turns down the noise so the real signal can get through.

You don't need to build a perfect system. You just need one that helps you pause before you absorb. That pause? That's where clarity lives.

If you're not curating your inputs, you're being shaped by them. And odds are, they weren't designed with your best thinking in mind.

Recognizing and Overcoming Cognitive Biases

Even the sharpest thinkers are skewed by something more powerful than misinformation: their own mental shortcuts.

You can filter out the noise, structure your tasks, and build the perfect decision-making system, but if you don't account for bias, you're still steering by a bent compass. The error isn't in the map, it's in the way you're reading it. The distortion is embedded in how you process reality.

Cognitive bias is not a character flaw. It's a feature of the human brain. Your mind evolved to conserve energy, not to be objectively correct. So when your brain faces uncertainty, it doesn't wait for full context. It fills in gaps. Guesses. Then quietly files those guesses under facts.

The result? You don't think through data. You think around it, subconsciously framing it to confirm what you already believe.

The Most Common Mental Landmines

Here are the mental landmines most likely to trip you up. There are dozens of cognitive biases, but these are the ones that derail clear thinking most consistently in fast-paced professional environments.

- Confirmation Bias

You look for evidence that supports your belief and ignore what contradicts it. It happens during hiring decisions, product evaluations, even brainstorming. Once your brain likes an idea, it goes shopping for reasons to keep liking it.

- Anchoring Bias

You rely too heavily on the first piece of information you receive, even when it's irrelevant. Salary negotiations, client contracts, strategic planning, all of these are prone to anchoring. That first number, deadline, or benchmark becomes a mental anchor. Everything else gets adjusted around it, even when it shouldn't.

- Availability Heuristic

If something comes to mind quickly, you assume it's more common, more important, or more true. This is why anecdotal horror stories carry more weight than statistical facts. You got one complaint. And it rattled you more than thirty days of quiet success. That's availability bias at work.

- Sunk Cost Fallacy

You've already invested time, money, or energy into something, so you keep going, even when it's clearly not working. This bias ruins careers, clogs backlogs, and drags teams down paths they should've abandoned months ago.

- Overconfidence Effect

You overestimate your knowledge, your memory, or your accuracy, especially when stakes are high. This shows up as premature decisions, flawed assumptions, and underestimating complexity.

That's not arrogance. It's architecture, your brain's default shortcut for reducing doubt when certainty feels safer than accuracy.

The Real-World Impact of Bias

Let's say you're leading a product launch. You've got a promising idea, strong team momentum, and positive feedback from early testers. You're excited. Everyone's aligned. But here's what might be happening under the surface:

- You dismiss negative feedback as "edge cases." (confirmation bias)

- You rely on pricing models from your last launch without rechecking market conditions. (anchoring)

- You ignore new data that contradicts your original assumptions. (sunk cost fallacy)

- You assume success because your closest competitor pulled it off. (availability heuristic)

- You overestimate your team's readiness to scale. (overconfidence effect)

The outcome? You launch a product that was never properly tested, budgeted, or timed. The failure feels like bad luck. But it wasn't. It was baked into the thinking.

Spotting the Bias in the Moment

You can't eliminate bias, but you can interrupt it. That's the real skill. Build systems that catch your shortcuts before they become bad decisions.

Here's how:

1. Bias Checklists

Create a short list of questions to review before major decisions:

- What am I assuming?

- What evidence am I ignoring?

- What's the first piece of data I anchored to?

- What would I do if I hadn't already invested X in this?

- Who disagrees with me, and why?

Use it in team meetings. Use it alone. The act of asking slows the cognitive shortcut.

2. Devil's Advocate Protocol

Assign someone (or yourself) the role of challenger. Not to be contrary, but to deliberately hunt for holes in your thinking. Make it procedural, not personal. Do this before every high-stakes pitch, proposal, or pivot.

3. Pre-Mortems

Instead of asking, "What could go wrong?" try this:

- "It's six months from now and this decision failed. Why?"

List every plausible cause. This bypasses the ego's need to defend and lets you explore risks more honestly.

4. Base Rate Awareness

Ask: What's the average outcome for situations like this? Strip away uniqueness and look at category data. How often do new ventures succeed? How long do typical integrations take? What's the average sales cycle? Anchor in reality, not exceptions.

5. Red Teaming

In high-stakes environments (think: military, cybersecurity), red teams are used to simulate the enemy. Apply this logic to your own planning. Build a mini-red team to break your plan before reality does. It's less fun, but far cheaper than a real failure.

Bias in Personal Context

Bias isn't just a business problem. It shows up in how you read people, how you remember events, even how you judge your own emotions.

Let's say a coworker misses a deadline. You instantly think: lazy. Disengaged. Irresponsible.

You don't pause to consider: sick kid? Overlapping project? Bottleneck outside their control?

That's attribution bias. And if you're not careful, it builds resentment based on faulty conclusions. Bias erodes not just thinking, but relationships, because it blinds you to context.

Building Cognitive Humility

The goal isn't to become cold or hyperrational. It's to develop a kind of internal honesty, where you recognize that your brain is a pattern-seeking machine, not a truth-seeking one. It feels good to be right. It feels better to be curious.

Start defaulting to uncertainty with intention. Let people surprise you. Let data override instinct. Let feedback sting a little without turning it into shame.

You won't always catch your biases in real time. But if you build a habit of reflection and use tools that challenge automatic thinking, you'll start noticing the patterns that used to slip by unnoticed.

That's the beginning of sharper thought. Not more knowledge. More clarity about how your own mind works.

Understanding Logical Fallacies in Everyday Thinking

Fallacies aren't just the domain of bad-faith arguments online. They sneak into your reasoning more often than you'd like to admit. Probably without realizing it.

They slip in when you're trying to prove a point, defend your choices, or win an argument you're not emotionally ready to lose. They pretend to be logic, but they're mental shortcuts in disguise, cloaking emotion in argument. And they can cost you credibility, even when your instincts are right.

If cognitive bias is the internal distortion in how you interpret information, logical fallacies are the external distortion in how you present it.

They break arguments. They damage trust. And they dilute your message by making you sound more defensive than persuasive.

Why Fallacies Stick (Even When You Know Better)

You've probably heard some of the classics: straw man, slippery slope, ad hominem. You might have even learned the terms back in school. But here's the kicker: knowledge doesn't equal immunity. Most fallacies aren't committed because someone's dumb. They're committed because someone's rushed, cornered, or emotionally overcommitted.

You fall back on faulty logic when:

- You want to win, not understand.

- You fire back before you think.

- And if the stakes feel personal, logic takes a back seat.

- You're tired, reactive, or under social pressure.

Recognizing fallacies isn't about pedantic argument policing. It's about protecting clarity. Because once your reasoning is infected, it doesn't matter how good your point is, no one will trust it.

The Fallacies That Derail Professionals Most Often

Let's look at the real-world offenders. Just the ones that show up in meetings, pitches, negotiations, and difficult conversations.

1. The Straw Man

During the Q2 planning session, someone panicked: *So we're ignoring the budget now?*

That wasn't the proposal. That was the straw man talking.

2. The False Dilemma (Either/Or)

You frame things in black and white when reality has shades of gray.

"We either launch now, or we lose the market."
Not necessarily. There may be staggered options, beta rollouts, or competitor delays you haven't considered.

3. The Slippery Slope

You argue that one step will inevitably lead to catastrophe.

"If we let the client revise the contract, they'll walk all over us."
Maybe. Or maybe they just need one clause updated. Fear-based forecasting isn't logic.

4. The Ad Hominem

You attack the person instead of addressing their argument.

"Of course he disagrees, he's always been a pessimist."
Even pessimists can be right. If your point only works by discrediting the speaker, it's not a strong point.

5. The Appeal to Authority

You cite credentials or popularity instead of evidence.

"This approach is backed by top industry experts."

Impressive title. Now let's see if the evidence matches. Authority doesn't guarantee accuracy.

6. The Circular Argument

You assume the conclusion within the premise.

"We can't change the policy because it's always been our policy."
That's not an argument. That's inertia.

7. The Hasty Generalization

You jump to conclusions based on too little evidence.

"That one client hated it, so this strategy is clearly flawed."
That's one data point, not a trend.

8. The Appeal to Emotion

You use feelings in place of logic.

"Think of how bad we'll feel if we don't act now."
Emotions can inform values, but they can't replace reasoning.

These fallacies aren't just theoretical problems. They affect real decisions. They turn strategic discussions into emotional battles. They make meetings feel adversarial instead of productive.

How to Catch Yourself in the Act

You won't always catch fallacies as you're speaking. But you can train yourself to notice patterns.

1. Slow Down the Claim

Before you argue a point, pause and ask:

- Is this based on evidence, or am I just repeating what feels true?

2. Reframe the Pushback

If someone disagrees, try restating their position neutrally, without sarcasm, exaggeration, or assumptions.

If you can't restate it fairly, you're probably arguing with a straw man.

3. Audit Your Own Rhetoric

After a high-stakes discussion, do a post-mortem. Not just on what was said, but how. Where did logic hold? Where did emotion hijack the wheel?

4. Develop a "Check Engine" Light

Fallacies often follow internal signals: frustration, impatience, defensiveness. Notice those spikes. They're usually where the logic goes soft.

What Clear Argument Looks Like

It's not flashy. It's not emotionally manipulative. It doesn't rely on credentials or volume. It's calm, structured, and transparent.

"I'm recommending Option B because it aligns with our objectives, minimizes cost risk, and offers measurable ROI. I understand the concerns about timeline, and I've run scenarios where we mitigate that through phased implementation."

No hyperbole. No character attacks. No fear tactics. Just structured thought, spoken with respect.

This is how people who actually get heard communicate. Not louder. Cleaner.

When to Call It Out, and When to Let It Go

There's a temptation, once you understand fallacies, to call them out everywhere. Don't. It's not productive. It's smug.

If someone uses faulty logic in good faith, ask questions. Let them walk themselves toward clarity. If they're arguing in bad faith, correcting the fallacy won't fix the dynamic. Walk away or refocus on your own clarity.

You don't need to "win" the argument. You need to stay grounded in your thinking. That's the only real win.

Practical Frameworks for Enhanced Decision-Making

Confidence wavers under pressure. Clarity when things get tight is what actually holds.

When pressure hits, deadlines, conflicting priorities, limited data, your brain reaches for shortcuts. It's instinct. But instinctive thinking rarely produces strategic results. It leads to overcommitment, risk avoidance, and whatever feels safest in the moment.

You don't need more intuition. You need a structure that holds up when your instincts are scrambled.

This is where frameworks come in. They don't make decisions for you. They expose your thinking, so you can see what you're actually choosing.

What a Framework Really Is

Forget the consultant-speak. A framework lays out a decision. It stops it from spinning in your head. It turns invisible tension into visible tradeoffs.

Used well, a framework:

- Forces clarity and exposes where you're rushing or blind.

- Creates a paper trail for why you chose what you did.

You're not outsourcing your judgment. You're scaffolding it.

Let's walk through four frameworks that work in the real world, under stress, in motion, and when stakes are high.

1. The Pros and Cons List (Upgraded)

Yes, it's basic. That's the point. It gives you a fast, frictionless way to get ideas out of your head and onto paper. But most people stop too early.

The upgrade? Weigh it. Rank it. Force tradeoffs.

Don't just list, rank. Score each point 1 to 5. Then check the shape, not just the score.

This method makes patterns visible. Sometimes the "con" column is longer, but weaker. Or a single "pro" outweighs the rest. Don't let the math make the call. Let it test whether your gut's bluffing.

Use when: You're choosing between two known paths and need to untangle emotional fog.

2. SWOT Analysis (Strengths, Weaknesses, Opportunities, Threats)

Originally built for strategic planning, SWOT works just as well on personal or team-level decisions.

- Strengths – Internal advantages

- Weaknesses – Internal gaps or risks

- Opportunities – External trends you can leverage

- Threats – External forces that might undercut you

Let's say you're debating a career pivot. SWOT makes it visible:

- Your strength is adaptability.

- Your weakness is lack of industry knowledge.

- Your opportunity is a market trend you're ahead of.

- Your threat is financial instability during the transition.

It's no longer a foggy hunch. It's a terrain you can plan against. With friction points you can address instead of avoiding.

Use when: You need to zoom out and look at internal vs. external forces.

3. Six Thinking Hats (Edward de Bono)

This one's deceptively powerful. It's not a group gimmick, it's a way to separate modes of thinking so you stop mixing logic with fear, or creativity with judgment.

Each hat forces a mental switch so you stop blending instinct with strategy:

- White Hat – Facts and data

- Red Hat – Emotions and intuition

- Black Hat – Caution and criticism

- Yellow Hat – Optimism and potential

- Green Hat – Creativity and alternatives

- Blue Hat – Process and structure

You can do this solo or with a team. Run through each hat in sequence. Give each lens a few minutes. No cross-talk. No argument.

The magic isn't in the hats. It's in the containment. You give every mode of thinking its turn, without letting any one dominate too early.

Use when: You're overthinking or stuck in loops, especially in group dynamics.

4. The Eisenhower Matrix

You've probably seen the grid. It works because most people confuse urgency with importance.

Two axis:

- Urgent vs. Not Urgent

- Important vs. Not Important

Which gives you four quadrants:

- Do Now – Urgent + Important

- Schedule – Not Urgent + Important

- Delegate – Urgent + Not Important

- Eliminate – Not Urgent + Not Important

This tool isn't just for to-do lists. It's a mindset audit. What are you reacting to because it's noisy? What have you postponed because it's quiet but crucial?

Use when: You're overwhelmed and can't figure out where to start.

Choosing the Right Tool for the Moment

Don't try to force every decision into a framework. That's just another form of procrastination. Instead, pay attention to the signal:

- Feeling foggy? → Use the pros and cons upgrade.

- Facing strategic complexity? → Try SWOT.

- Overthinking or group paralysis? → Deploy the Six Hats.

- Drowning in tasks? → Sort with the Eisenhower Matrix.

None of these tools will make your decision. But they'll strip away the clutter so you can make it with intention, not inertia.

Why Frameworks Outperform Instinct Under Pressure

Instinct is useful. But under stress, instinct becomes bias. And bias, left unchecked, makes you double down on the familiar, avoid risk, or chase speed at the cost of accuracy.

Frameworks don't eliminate pressure. They organize it. They put your thoughts where you can see them. They create space between the impulse and the action.

That space? That's where better choices live.

Developing a Balanced Mindset for Rational and Emotional Insight

Rationality and emotion aren't enemies. Treating them that way is the real error.

The idea that emotion clouds logic is outdated, and wrong. What actually clouds logic is unacknowledged emotion. Ignored emotion doesn't vanish. It reroutes showing up as self-sabotage or misplaced certainty. It's not rage that wrecks decisions, it's the fear you're pretending isn't there.

If you want to make better decisions, solve harder problems, and communicate more clearly, you need both systems online, your reasoning and your emotional intelligence.

This isn't about being "soft." It's about being calibrated.

The False Divide: Emotion vs. Logic

Let's clear this up.

- Logic asks, "What's true?"

- Emotion asks, "What matters?"

Both are necessary. Logic gives you the terrain. But emotion? It's how you decide which risks are worth the climb.

When people say "be objective," what they usually mean is "suppress your response." But pure objectivity doesn't exist. Even your definition of a good outcome is shaped by personal values. Even your risk tolerance is emotional.

So the goal isn't to remove emotion. It's to integrate it consciously, to use it as signal, not sabotage.

What Emotional Intelligence Actually Looks Like

It's not about being nice. It's about being aware and responsive, to yourself, to others, to the context.

Emotionally intelligent thinkers:

- Notice their internal state before it spills into action.

- Can pause and ask, "Is this feeling useful or just familiar?"

- Handle friction without making it personal.

- Stay curious when triggered, instead of reactive.

You can develop emotional intelligence the same way you develop any other skill, through awareness, reflection, and practice. It starts by noticing the signals before they become symptoms.

Three Mindset Shifts That Build Balance

You don't need a total personality overhaul. You need to shift a few key defaults.

1. Replace Control with Clarity

Trying to control emotions, yours or others', only works until pressure hits. Then the mask cracks.

Instead: name what's happening. Not in therapy-speak. Just honest labeling.

- *"I'm anxious because this feels risky."*

- *"I'm irritated because my idea wasn't acknowledged."*

- *"I'm withdrawn because I'm afraid of being wrong."*

Clarity disarms emotion's grip. It turns the feeling from threat into data.

2. Replace Judgment with Curiosity

When emotion shows up, especially in others, your instinct might be to dismiss, fix, or argue. But that kills dialogue.

Instead: pause and ask questions.

- *"What's behind this reaction?"*

- *"Is there a past pattern shaping this moment?"*

- *"What might I be missing in their perspective?"*

Curiosity lowers the stakes. It buys you space to think before you retaliate.

3. Replace Performance with Presence

You don't need to look unshakeable. You need to be real, with boundaries.

Instead of posturing:

- *"I'm not sure yet, but I'm thinking it through."*

- *"I hear where you're coming from, and I'm weighing it seriously."*

- *"That reaction surprised me. Can we slow it down?"*

Presence means you're in the moment, not overcompensating for it. That builds trust, and keeps your own system from flooding.

Tools That Support the Balance

Skip the hours of meditation. You need friction-tested tools that work fast.

- Mindfulness Micro-Pauses

Before key decisions or responses, take ten seconds. Three deep breaths. Ask:

"What's driving me right now, fear, ego, clarity, care?"

You'd be shocked how many choices are driven by the first two.

- Journaling for Pattern Recognition

Not for venting. For learning. After stressful moments, write:

- What triggered me?

- What story did I tell myself?

- What's the actual story?

Do this weekly. You'll see patterns. That's where growth lives.

- Somatic Awareness

Emotions show up in the body first. Tight jaw. Shallow breath. Clenched fists.

Catch the signal, trace it back to the thought. You'll start spotting reactions before they hijack your logic.

- Emotional Vocabulary Upgrade

Replace "stressed" with something more precise: irritated, ashamed, uncertain, restless. Language sharpens perception. Perception drives response.

Integration in Action: A Real-Life Moment

Darren, a department head in a high-growth startup, found himself constantly battling his COO in meetings. Every idea he pitched was met with resistance. He chalked it up to personality clash.

But after running a brief post-meeting analysis using the journaling tool, he spotted the trigger: the COO's tone activated a childhood wound around not being heard. Darren wasn't reacting to the ideas. He was reacting to an old script.

The next week, he prepared by naming the emotion ("I'm bracing for dismissal") and rehearsed neutral, clarifying questions to stay grounded. The shift wasn't dramatic, but it was immediate. Less defensiveness. More strategic pushback. Better outcomes.

Logic didn't fix that meeting. Emotional awareness did.

The Outcome of Balance

A balanced mindset doesn't mean neutral. It means responsive. Not driven by habit. Not hijacked by fear. Just attuned, steady, and sharp.

You won't get it perfect. But the goal isn't perfection, it's traction. It's the ability to pivot mid-thought, mid-sentence, mid-conflict. To re-center yourself before you cause a chain reaction you didn't intend.

Critical thinking doesn't happen in a vacuum. It happens inside human systems, driven by values, stories, and nervous systems. The more you understand those systems, especially your own, the less likely you are to mistake reaction for reasoning.

Tools for Effective Prioritization in a Fast-Paced World

In the real world, prioritization doesn't happen on a whiteboard. It happens in the middle of chaos, three deadlines, two Slack pings, one client meltdown, and a calendar that looks like it lost a bet.

Everyone talks about "working smarter." But no one tells you how to choose which smart work actually matters. That's where critical thinking meets real-world triage.

Prioritization isn't just time management. It's strategic energy deployment. It's about knowing what deserves your full attention, what can run on autopilot, and what should be ruthlessly ignored.

Let's get tactical.

Why Urgency Wins (And How to Fight Back)

Your brain is biased toward immediacy. That's why a blinking notification can hijack your day faster than a long-term goal ever will. Urgency feels important, even when it's not.

This is how you end up spending a Tuesday rearranging icons in a project management app while your biggest proposal goes untouched. You're busy. But not effective.

To break the cycle, you need tools that:

- Shrink your focus.

- Surface what matters now.

- Put limits around what doesn't.

Here are the ones that actually work when your week's on fire.

1. The Daily 3

Every morning (or the night before), identify:

- 1 thing that must get done today.

- 1 thing that moves a key project forward.

- 1 thing that's optional, but valuable.

This isn't a to-do list. It's a priority spotlight.

If everything on your calendar gets canceled, these are the three you still do. No excuses. No reschedules.

Why it works: It filters noise, reinforces momentum, and gives you small wins even when the day derails.

2. The ABCDE Method

Popularized by Brian Tracy, this tool forces prioritization by consequence, not just convenience.

- A – Must do: severe consequences if not completed

- B – Should do: mild consequences

- C – Nice to do: no consequences

- D – Delegate: someone else can handle it

- E – Eliminate: it doesn't need to exist

Don't just label. Take action:

- Do all A's first.

- Only move to B's when A's are done.

- Never touch C's until B's are cleared.

- D and E? Clear them fast.

Why it works: It removes ambiguity and gives guilt-free permission to drop low-value tasks.

3. Time Blocking

Take your calendar. Assign every block of time to a task, meeting, or buffer. No empty space. No mystery gaps.

But here's the trick most people miss: schedule your high-cognition work during your personal peak energy window, not when your calendar happens to be open.

Whether that's 8am or 11pm, block it and defend it.

Also: leave white space. Context switching kills momentum. Give yourself buffer between meetings or deep work sprints so you don't burn out your cognitive fuel by noon.

Why it works: It turns priorities into appointments, not wishes.

4. The "Hell Yes or Later" Rule

If you're overwhelmed with tasks, requests, and invitations, use this filter:

- Is this a clear "hell yes"?

- If not, it's a no, for now.

This applies to:

- Volunteering for new projects

- Accepting client work

- Taking meetings

- Reading that article someone sent you

You can revisit it later. But if it's not a priority now, it doesn't get airtime.

Why it works: It prevents emotional overcommitment and keeps your "yes" powerful.

5. Task Batching + Themed Days

Instead of bouncing between unrelated tasks, batch similar ones into chunks:

- Respond to all messages in a 45-minute block.

- Schedule creative work (writing, strategy) for mornings.

- Use Friday afternoons for cleanup and admin.

You can also try themed days:

- Mondays = strategy

- Tuesdays = meetings

- Wednesdays = creation

- Thursdays = delivery

- Fridays = admin + reset

Why it works: Reduces mental load and preserves flow by limiting task-switching.

When Priorities Collide: Use the Triage Lens

Sometimes, everything does feel urgent. That's when triage thinking kicks in. It's not pretty, but it's essential.

Ask:

- What happens if I don't do this today?

- Who is actually impacted, and how badly?

- What's the cost of delay?

- Can I delegate, defer, or do it faster without damaging the outcome?

This aims to reduce damage without turning against yourself. Perfection has nothing to do with it.

If you can't do everything, don't. Do the work that moves the needle, not just the work that's yelling the loudest.

Kill Your Darlings (Yes, Even the Smart Ones)

One of the hardest parts of prioritization isn't saying no to bad ideas, it's letting go of good ones that just don't belong right now.

You might have a killer pitch, a beautiful deck, or a promising strategy. But if it doesn't align with this quarter's focus, it's a distraction.

Capture it. Save it. But don't chase it.

You're not here to collect clever ideas. You're here to deliver meaningful results.

Make Prioritization a Daily Practice

You don't need a perfect productivity system. You need a simple ritual that keeps you from falling back into reaction mode.

That might look like:

- 10 minutes of planning each morning

- 30 minutes of weekly review every Friday

- 2 resets during the day (after lunch, before shutdown)

Check your top 3. Recalibrate your time blocks. Let go of what no longer fits.

Because here's the truth: most people don't fail for lack of time. They fail for lack of clarity.

Build the Foundations, One Filter at a Time

By now, you've built six core muscles:

1. Filtering the flood of information before it drowns you.

2. Spotting the biases that twist your judgment.

3. Catching faulty logic before it collapses your argument.

4. Applying decision frameworks when your brain panics.

5. Aligning emotional insight with structured thought.

6. Protecting your time from urgency inflation.

These aren't magic tricks. They're leverage points. And when practiced together, they make your thinking sharper, not just smarter.

In the next chapter, we'll level up again: deeper problem-solving models, emotional integration under stress, and the kind of clarity you can defend in any room, at any speed.

2

Advanced Problem-Solving Strategies

Integrating Emotional Intelligence into Rational Problem Solving

We tend to treat emotion and logic like rival forces in a courtroom. One argues, the other interrupts. One plans, the other panics. But high-stakes problem solving doesn't reward this courtroom metaphor. The people who thrive under pressure, navigate conflict, or make sharp decisions in uncertain conditions have figured something out: emotional intelligence isn't the opposite of rational thinking. It's the stabilizer that keeps logic from tipping into panic, bias, or paralysis.

Emotion Is Not the Enemy, Poor Integration Is

Let's be clear: emotion isn't the problem. What derails us is the misplacement of emotion. We minimize or ignore signals until they erupt. Or we get flooded by those signals and mistake them for data. That's how people lose their edge, by confusing urgency with importance, discomfort with danger, or confidence with correctness.

Emotionally intelligent thinkers don't suppress their reactions. They track them. They use them to inform decisions. That distinction matters. When Elena, a mid-level manager in a healthcare startup, faced a critical decision about laying off staff during a budget crisis, she didn't default to numbers alone. She identified her guilt and anxiety, acknowledged their presence, and then used those emotions to probe deeper. Why was she avoiding a direct conversation with her team? What assumptions was she making about their resilience or her own role as a leader? That reflection didn't stop her from acting, it sharpened her strategy. She delivered the news with empathy and gave her team control over how the changes would roll out. The outcome? Higher morale than expected, and a faster recovery curve.

Emotional Literacy: The First Lever

Before emotional intelligence becomes useful, it has to become legible. Most people operate in a vague fog of "stress," "frustration," or "pressure." But problem solving requires precision. You can't adjust what you can't name.

Start here:

- Label your emotion in specific terms. Not "bad", but "resentful," "exposed," "resented," "cornered."

- Check for origin. Ask: Is this emotion about this moment, or is it echoing a previous experience?

- Track intensity and trajectory. Is it building? Fading? Looping?

Emotional literacy allows you to put data around your reactions. You're not being soft. You're mapping your inner feedback system instead of crashing into it at full speed.

The Moment Before You React: A Tactical Pause

In most problem-solving scenarios, the moment that matters isn't the one where you speak, it's the one before. That tiny space between impulse and action is where critical damage, or brilliant clarity, happens.

Developing a "pause reflex" gives your brain room to integrate emotional input before it becomes behavioral output. Here's how to build it:

- Name what you feel. (*"I'm angry. I'm also nervous this won't work."*)

- Acknowledge what you want to do. (*"I want to shut this down and walk away."*)

- Question the outcome. (*"Will that move the issue forward, or just protect me?"*)

This three-step loop takes less than 10 seconds. But in high-pressure meetings, difficult conversations, or personal crises, it can change the trajectory of your entire decision path.

Bias and Emotion: Unholy Allies

One of the trickiest aspects of emotional intelligence is recognizing when your emotions are reinforcing existing cognitive biases. Think of it this way: your brain likes shortcuts. Emotion gives those shortcuts fuel. That's how confirmation bias, sunk cost fallacy, and groupthink get past your filters.

Let's say you're in a product strategy meeting. You feel strongly that a feature idea is weak, but your boss loves it. You already have data to show it underperforms. Still, you find yourself biting your tongue. Why?

- Fear of disapproval?

- Conflict avoidance?

- Loyalty to your boss's past successes?

Emotion isn't just about what we feel about a problem. It affects what we feel safe to say, believe, or challenge. To counteract this:

- Use "emotion audits" before and after major decisions. Write down what you felt, what action you took, and what alternative actions you considered but dismissed.

- Name the bias likely involved. Then question its influence.

- Run the same scenario through a different emotional lens. If you were calm, curious, or detached, what would you see?

Emotional Intelligence in Group Dynamics

Problem solving rarely happens in a vacuum. You're not just managing your own emotions, you're interpreting others', navigating egos, and trying to keep a team moving toward a solution without imploding.

This is where many rational thinkers fail. They come prepared with logic and walk into a room filled with subtext. The smartest idea in the room doesn't always win. The emotionally legible one does.

That's not a call to dumb things down. It's a prompt to match communication with emotional tone. For example:

Instead of: *"Here's the most efficient plan."*

Try: *"I know everyone's stretched thin right now, but here's a plan that could lighten the load and get results faster."*

Same logic. More connection.

If you want your ideas to land in high-stress rooms, they need to feel like relief, not challenge.

The Payoff: Cleaner Thinking, Stronger Solutions

When you develop emotional intelligence as part of your critical thinking toolkit, you gain something most people miss, a feedback loop that corrects you in real time. You stop doubling down on bad calls just to save face. You notice when you're spiraling instead of solving. You recover faster when plans go sideways.

Emotion, when integrated, helps you see problems more fully. It makes you braver when the stakes are high, clearer when the fog sets in, and sharper when you need to lead others through chaos.

That's not softness. That's strength calibrated by insight.

Leveraging Technology for Smarter Problem Solving

Technology isn't the answer to every problem, but it's a lever. And when you're buried in complexity, urgency, or sheer volume, the right tool doesn't just make things easier, it changes the shape of the problem itself. Professionals stuck in reactive loops often blame themselves for inefficiency when the real issue is a failure to offload the cognitive load. Technology, used well, doesn't replace thinking. It frees it.

Smart problem-solvers use tech as an extension of their mental capacity. Not as a crutch, not as a distraction, and definitely not as a substitute for judgment. The key is integration, building workflows where tools enhance awareness, accelerate analysis, and support better decisions without introducing more noise.

Start with what tech is good at: pattern recognition, task automation, data synthesis, and reducing friction. Then apply it with discipline. Most people jump from one app to the next hoping a new interface will fix their disorganization. It won't. What will: using the right tool, for the right purpose, at the right point in your decision cycle.

Start by asking three questions:

- What type of problem am I solving: task-based, analytical, strategic, or interpersonal?

- What parts of this process are repeatable, measurable, or prone to error?

- What decisions am I making based on assumptions I could verify with better data?

Once you've mapped that landscape, you can bring in the tech. Here's how.

Task-based problems call for automation. Think: scheduling, reminders, document sharing, cross-functional updates. Tools like Trello, Notion, or Asana aren't just for teams, they're for brains that need visual structure and real-time progress tracking. If your working memory is stretched thin, don't try to fix it with willpower. Fix it with systems.

Analytical problems need data support. Whether you're reviewing marketing metrics or running an A/B test, tools like Tableau, Power BI, or even Excel's lesser-known functions (like Power Query or Solver) give you leverage. The critical shift isn't collecting data, it's being able to explore it without drowning in it. Dashboards beat reports. Filters beat long meetings. Visual patterns beat rows of decimals.

Strategic problems benefit from modeling tools. When outcomes are high-stakes or long-term, don't rely on whiteboards. Build simulations. Use mind mapping software to visualize cascading effects. Try scenario planning templates to test outcomes. Apps like Miro, Lucidchart, or even simple decision-tree builders can help you clarify assumptions before they harden into commitments.

Interpersonal problems? Use tech to enhance, not avoid, communication. Tools like Loom for asynchronous clarity, Slack for clean thread separation, and AI-assisted writing aids like Grammarly or ChatGPT can help polish tone without losing authenticity. But remember, no tool replaces trust. If you're using technology to dodge uncomfortable conversations, you're solving the wrong problem.

The danger, of course, is overreliance. When people say they're overwhelmed by digital tools, they often mean they've lost the plot. Too many dashboards. Too many notifications. Too many systems to check. The solution isn't more tech. It's better curation.

Use this rule: no more than three core tools per problem domain. For project management, one dashboard. For team communication, one channel. For data analysis, one interface. Complexity compounds when we confuse optional features with necessary inputs.

Also important: tech isn't neutral. Every platform embeds assumptions. About time, value, visibility, and control. For example, tools that reward responsiveness over thoughtfulness can warp team culture. Apps that track productivity without context can penalize deep work. Good problem solvers pay attention to those cues. They use the tech, but they don't let it use them.

One often-overlooked category is cognitive support. Mindset tools. Burnout trackers. Apps that monitor energy cycles, not just time blocks. If you know that your decision quality drops by 3 p.m., build systems that flag high-stakes choices before then. Use time-tracking tools not just to log hours, but to study your own patterns of attention, drift, and resistance.

And then there's AI. Generative tools are exploding, text, image, code, simulation. You don't need to become an AI expert. But you do need to test what it can and can't do for your workflows. If it saves you three hours a week, that's not just convenience. That's strategic margin, time you can reallocate to deeper analysis or human-centered work that machines still can't do well.

But don't let the algorithm lead. AI is a suggestion engine, not a thinking substitute. The best results come from people who use these tools to surface options, then sharpen them with judgment. Feed it smart prompts. Challenge its assumptions. Cross-check its logic. That's how technology becomes an amplifier, not a liability.

The final skill here is subtraction. Knowing when to cut tools. Reclaim mental bandwidth. Re-simplify a system that's gotten too clever for its own good. That takes humility. But it's part of what separates the digitally competent from the strategically sharp.

Technology won't solve your problem for you. But if you pair it with clarity, restraint, and sharp emotional tracking, it can lift the mental weight that keeps most people spinning. It's not just about speed. It's about making sure your energy goes where it counts.

Overcoming Fear of Failure with Robust Decision Frameworks

Most people don't freeze because they don't know what to do. They freeze because they're afraid of what happens if they do the wrong thing. Fear of failure is the invisible bottleneck in decision-making. It slows smart people down. It turns options into threats. And it creates the illusion that the safest move is no move at all.

But fear doesn't disappear by logic alone. You can't out-think it, you have to out-structure it. Decision frameworks offer that scaffolding, flexible enough to handle uncertainty without letting you collapse under it.

The goal isn't to eliminate risk. It's to shrink the shadow it casts.

Start with this: failure isn't a full stop. It's a data point. But most people don't see it that way. They see it as identity collapse. If I fail, I'm incompetent. If I'm wrong, I lose credibility. If this doesn't work, I'm exposed. That mindset turns even small decisions into ego landmines.

You can interrupt that pattern by using frameworks that externalize the process. A strong decision structure shifts the focus from *What if I mess up?* to *What conditions are present, what tradeoffs exist, and what does the path forward look like, win or lose?*

One of the most versatile tools is the WRAP model, developed by Chip and Dan Heath. It stands for:

- Widen your options

- Reality-test your assumptions

- Attain distance before deciding

- Prepare to be wrong

Let's break it down.

Widen your options forces you out of the trap of binary thinking. Most people collapse every problem into two choices, usually opposites. Stay or go. Launch or kill. But better decisions almost always emerge when you push for at least a third path. Try this: ask, *"What would I do if neither of these were allowed?"* or *"How would I advise a friend in my position?"*

Reality-test your assumptions requires you to stop arguing with your own echo chamber. Instead of looking for more data to support what you already want to do, try what's called a disconfirming test. Ask: *"What would have to be true for the opposite of my preferred choice to be the better one?"* Then test that. Go talk to someone who disagrees with you, not to debate them, but to understand the logic they're using.

Attain distance before deciding inserts time between reaction and commitment. When you're emotionally flooded, your brain narrows. Fear turns your timeline into a countdown. But unless the building's on fire, urgency is often a distortion. Try the **10/10/10 rule**: How will I feel about this decision 10 minutes from now, 10 months from now, and 10 years from now? The goal isn't to predict your feelings perfectly. It's to stretch your time horizon enough to clear the fog.

Prepare to be wrong sounds defeatist, but it's the opposite. It's how you reclaim control in uncertainty. You're not betting your identity on being right. You're planning for multiple outcomes. Create a **premortem**: a reverse failure analysis. Imagine that your decision led to disaster. What went wrong? What signals did you miss? Then use that insight to build early-warning systems or mitigation strategies into your plan.

That process doesn't just reduce failure, it redefines it. Because even when a choice goes sideways, you've already thought through contingencies. That's resilience by design, not accident.

Another useful structure is the **Decision Matrix**, especially when comparing options with multiple variables. List your choices across the top. Criteria down the side. Weight each factor based on its importance. Score each option. Then step back and look at the pattern. This doesn't pretend everything can be quantified. It reveals what you're privileging without realizing it.

Let's say you're deciding between two job offers. One has better pay, the other better work-life balance. You value both. But without a framework, you're stuck cycling through the same thoughts. With a matrix, you can see how much you're weighting flexibility versus salary. You might realize that your fear of turning down money is masking your deeper need for autonomy.

This is where decision-making and emotional intelligence collide. Frameworks only work if you're honest about your inputs. If you distort your priorities to protect your ego, the framework can't help you. But if you bring full clarity to the table, even when it's uncomfortable, you gain leverage.

You also gain momentum. Nothing slows growth like indecision masquerading as perfectionism. And that's what fear of failure really is: an attempt to find the perfect move so you never have to feel regret, embarrassment, or vulnerability. But the perfect move rarely exists. And when it does, it's only visible in hindsight.

The smartest professionals aren't fearless. They're failure-aware, but framework-protected. They don't wait for emotional certainty. They build process certainty. That's the shift.

So the next time you catch yourself stuck in mental loop-de-loops, ask:

- Have I clearly defined the actual decision I need to make?

- Have I explored more than two options?

- Have I tested my thinking against reality, not just instinct?

- Have I created distance from the emotional heat?

- Have I built a margin of error into my plan?

If the answer is yes, then move. Not because you're sure. But because you're structurally prepared to recover if you're wrong.

That's how you stop letting fear define the boundary of your action.

Creative Brainstorming Techniques for Innovative Solutions

Most brainstorming sessions are junk drawers. A few decent ideas buried under a pile of half-formed thoughts, forced enthusiasm, and awkward silences. People walk out smiling, then quietly revert to whatever they were doing before. Why? Because most brainstorming isn't structured to produce solutions. It's structured to avoid conflict, waste time, or show that everyone "contributed."

But real innovation doesn't come from open-ended chatter. It comes from constraint-driven friction, directional focus, and psychological safety. Their purpose is candor rather than comfort. If your process doesn't make room for discomfort, dissent, and divergence, you're not brainstorming. You're performing.

So stop asking people to "think outside the box" and start building boxes worth thinking inside.

The best creative thinking happens when boundaries are clear and stakes are high. Constraints create the need for innovation. Structure channels it. Here's how to lead or self-facilitate a brainstorming session that doesn't waste everyone's time.

Start with the **Problem Reframe**. Most sessions jump into solution mode too quickly. Instead, ask: *Are we solving the right problem?* Take the original problem statement and flip it:

"How do we boost engagement?" becomes *"Why are people disengaged?"*

"How do we cut costs?" becomes *"Where are we spending reactively instead of intentionally?"*

Even better: rephrase the problem from multiple stakeholder viewpoints. What does the user see? What does the client assume? What does the silent team member know that leadership doesn't? Framing is often where the creative leverage is hiding.

Next, apply **Divergent Thinking Windows**. These are short, timed intervals where quantity matters more than quality. You set a timer, say, five minutes, and generate as many ideas as possible without stopping. No critique. No explanation. Just output. The goal is to bypass your internal filter and force your brain past its first five obvious ideas.

Once the timer's up, pause. Then do it again, but this time with a constraint:

- Only solutions that require zero budget

- Only solutions that could be implemented in 72 hours

- Only solutions that involve breaking a rule

Constraints force novel thinking because they block your default pathways. That discomfort is where innovation lives.

After divergent rounds, move into **Pattern Recognition**. Cluster ideas by theme, approach, or impact level. This isn't about picking favorites. It's about seeing what your brain keeps circling. Patterns suggest pressure points. Outliers suggest blind spots.

Then comes **Constructive Destruction**. You take your best three ideas and actively try to break them. Ask:

- *What's the weak point?*

- *What assumption does this depend on?*

- *What would make this fail instantly in the real world?*

This isn't negativity, it's refinement. If your idea can't survive scrutiny, it's not ready. Better to kill it now than let the market do it for you later.

Finally, introduce **Role-Based Lenses**. Revisit top ideas from different perspectives:

- How would a customer experience this?

- How would a competitor respond to it?

- What would an intern, outsider, or child find confusing about it?

Each lens reveals different flaws, and sometimes, new strengths.

If you're solo-brainstorming, the process still applies. You're just switching roles internally. Write each perspective down. Don't rely on memory. The act of externalizing thought gives it shape. It also reveals where your thinking gets thin or repetitive.

Now let's talk tools. Tech can help, but it can't substitute for process. Use digital whiteboards (Miro, Mural, FigJam) to visually map clusters and track idea development over time. Use voice notes to capture fleeting thoughts during walks. Use templates for problem reframing or SCAMPER prompts (Substitute, Combine, Adapt, Modify, Put to another use, Eliminate, Reverse) to disrupt stale patterns.

But don't fall in love with novelty. Most great ideas are old ideas rearranged. Your job isn't to invent from scratch. It's to recombine what already exists into something that fits the current problem better than anything else.

That's why it's also crucial to separate **Idea Generation** from **Idea Selection**. Most teams rush to judgment because they're afraid of wasting time. But fast filtering kills weird ideas before they can mature. Let strange ideas breathe. Revisit them. See if they solve a problem you weren't consciously addressing. Innovation often hides in the idea that made everyone pause, but no one knew how to use yet.

And remember, creative solutions are often simple. Not easy. Simple. But simplicity takes work. It takes slicing away the clever parts that only exist to impress. It takes risk. You won't always get applause. But you will get clarity.

So the next time someone says "Let's brainstorm," don't roll your eyes. Lead. Set the boundaries. Introduce structure. Create friction. Pull the problem apart until something useful falls out. Then build around that.

That's what creative problem solving really is: less magic, more muscle.

Real-World Applications of Systems Thinking

When people hit a wall, they usually try to fix what's in front of them. Tweak a policy. Replace a person. Add a tool. But what they're actually responding to isn't a single point of failure, it's a ripple effect. One choice, feeding another. One constraint, creating a bottleneck downstream. And unless you can zoom out far enough to see the system, your fix becomes the next problem.

That's why systems thinking is essential. Not for theory. For traction.

Systems thinking isn't about mapping every possible connection in a mess of arrows and feedback loops. It's about shifting your attention from symptoms to structures. From moments to patterns. From parts to purpose. When you think in systems, you stop chasing short-term fixes and start designing long-term resilience.

The most practical application? **Diagnosing recurring problems.** When an issue resurfaces, project delays, customer churn, team burnout, it's rarely about one bad variable. It's about an invisible loop that keeps pulling you back to square one.

Take the classic example of a high-performing team that keeps burning out. Leadership responds by giving bonuses, wellness stipends, and occasional extra days off. Morale rises briefly, then crashes again. Why? Because the root issue isn't perks. It's a feedback loop of overcommitment, poor prioritization, and unclear boundaries.

In systems terms, the organization has created a reinforcing loop: overachievers take on too much, deliver results, get rewarded for speed, and are then expected to repeat the cycle. Until it breaks.

The solution isn't just to slow down. It's to break the loop. That might mean redefining metrics, changing incentive structures, or resetting cultural norms around availability. These aren't quick changes, but they're durable.

A second domain for systems thinking: **complex decision-making**. When you're weighing trade-offs across multiple layers, finance, ethics, operations, culture, you're not just solving for outcome A versus outcome B. You're solving for second- and third-order effects.

Let's say a nonprofit decides to launch a new service aimed at low-income families. The immediate goal is access. But what else changes? Does staff capacity shift? Does funding get reallocated? Does the new audience change the organization's identity over time?

Systems thinkers ask: What happens next? And then what?

This isn't paranoia. It's anticipation.

Here's a simple framework to apply:

1. **Identify the Elements**

What are the components of the system? This includes people, resources, policies, tools, and constraints.

2. **Map the Interactions**

What influences what? Draw the arrows. Identify feedback loops. Look for signs of escalation (reinforcing loops) or balance (balancing loops).

3. **Surface the Delays**

Most people underestimate time lags. A decision today might trigger outcomes next quarter. If you only measure immediate effects, you'll misdiagnose the system.

4. **Define the Goal of the System**

Every system has a purpose, whether stated or not. Sometimes what a system says it wants and what it actually produces are wildly different. Follow the outcomes.

5. **Look for Leverage Points**

Where can a small change produce a disproportionate effect? These are the points where intervention can break cycles or reset momentum.

For individual contributors and team leads, systems thinking often starts with workflow design. If your day is a blur of context-switching, dropped balls, and "urgent" fire drills, you're not just disorganized. You're inside a badly tuned system. And chances are, so is everyone else.

Instead of blaming time, start examining structure.

- Do roles have clarity, or does everyone guess?

- Do meetings create decisions, or delay them?

- Is responsibility distributed, or does it bottleneck?

Now apply the same mindset to personal growth. Let's say you're trying to build a new habit, writing daily, learning a language, managing stress. If it fails repeatedly, you don't need more discipline. You need to find the system around the behavior.

- What environmental cues support or sabotage the habit?

- What routines come before or after it?

- What feedback are you getting, reward, guilt, avoidance?

Change the system, not just the intention.

In high-stakes environments, emergency response, crisis management, product failure, systems thinking helps you triage without panic. You see where breakdowns are likely to cascade, where buffers exist, and where the system can self-correct if left alone.

But here's the catch: people resist systems thinking because it requires slowing down. Mapping, anticipating, zooming out, it all feels inefficient when pressure is on. But the cost of not doing it is worse. You fix the wrong part. You blame the wrong person. You repeat the same failure with more urgency and less clarity.

That's the difference between action and traction. Between chasing fires and redesigning the terrain.

The most effective leaders aren't the ones with the fastest answers. They're the ones who see the pattern before it repeats, and quietly reroute the system behind it.

Advanced Decision Models for High-Pressure Situations

When time is short and consequences are steep, people default to instinct. Sometimes that works. More often, it backfires. Because under pressure, instinct isn't neutral, it's skewed by adrenaline, fear, ego, or urgency. And what feels right in the moment might be exactly what locks you into a worse outcome later.

High-pressure situations demand more than fast thinking. They demand structured speed. That's what advanced decision models offer, not paralysis by analysis, but a mental scaffold to move fast and smart when it matters most.

Start with one of the most time-tested approaches: the **Recognition-Primed Decision Model (RPD)**. Originally developed from research with firefighters and military commanders, RPD explains how experienced decision-makers handle complex, time-sensitive choices without comparing endless options. They match patterns.

But here's the catch: pattern recognition only works if the patterns are valid. That requires experience, yes, but also post-action review. Debrief your calls. Study your mistakes. Learn what the right pattern feels like, not just what your gut tells you. Otherwise, you're just reinforcing bias with repetition.

The RPD model works best when:

- The environment is familiar or semi-familiar

- Time is constrained

- The cost of inaction is higher than the risk of an imperfect move

But it falls apart when you're in unknown terrain. That's when structured frameworks become essential.

One such model is the **OODA Loop**: Observe, Orient, Decide, Act. Created by U.S. Air Force strategist John Boyd, the OODA Loop drives more than decisions. It sustains tempo under pressure. In a high-pressure environment, speed isn't enough. You need to cycle through the loop faster and more accurately than your opponent, your obstacle, or your own self-doubt.

Break it down:

- Observe: Take in as much relevant information as possible. Situational awareness trumps gut reactions.

- Orient: Place what you're seeing in context. What's changed? What assumptions no longer hold?

- Decide: Pick a course of action, not forever, but for this loop.

- Act: Implement quickly, then prepare to re-loop.

The OODA Loop helps you avoid freezing or locking into a rigid plan. It's designed for dynamic environments, crises, negotiations, product launches, legal threats, where every decision shapes the field for the next one.

Another high-pressure model is **DECIDE**, often used in aviation:

- Detect the problem

- Estimate the need to react

- Choose a desirable outcome

- Identify actions to control the situation

- Do the necessary action

- Evaluate the effect of your action

DECIDE adds structure where the OODA loop emphasizes speed. It's slower, but thorough, ideal for situations where errors are catastrophic, like surgery, flight systems, or legal defense.

But most professionals aren't flying planes or disarming bombs. They're handling fast-moving, ambiguous business problems with interpersonal layers. For that, try **Pre-commitment Frameworks**. These are decisions made in advance, based on agreed-upon principles or thresholds.

For example:

- If our revenue drops below X, we cut Project Y, not head-count.

- If a partner misses three key deadlines, we renegotiate scope.

- If I hit decision fatigue by 6 p.m., I defer strategic choices until morning.

Pre-commitment cuts down on emotional reactivity. It turns pressure into action without requiring fresh judgment under stress. You're not being rigid. You're being pre-aligned with your own values and risk thresholds.

Another overlooked tactic in high-stakes decisions: **Decision Pre-Mortems**. Before you act, imagine the failure. Walk through the disaster scenario in detail. What went wrong? Where did you lose control? What assumptions fell apart?

Then reverse engineer safeguards. This builds resilience into your decision, not just logic. It also inoculates you against overconfidence, a major problem under pressure.

Now consider your **Decision Environment**. Are you solo? In a team? Facing a client? The model you use must match the decision dynamics.

- Solo, high-stakes: Use a hybrid of OODA and pre-mortem. Cycle fast but challenge your first instinct.

- Team, high-stakes: Use time-boxed DECIDE with clear roles. Assign one person to push back.

- Political, high-stakes: Layer in stakeholder mapping. Who has the most at stake emotionally, not just functionally?

And remember: speed is a function of preparation. The more you front-load your principles, pre-wire your thresholds, and rehearse your loops, the less you'll hesitate when the heat hits.

Pressure doesn't create clarity. It distorts it. But the right models give you guardrails. They turn fear into focus. Not because the risk disappears, but because you've already accounted for it.

In the end, high-pressure decision-making isn't about being fearless. It's about being pre-structured. That's what gives you the ability to move decisively when everyone else is stuck guessing, explaining, or blaming.

3

Enhancing Communication and Articulation Skills

Strategies for Presenting Ideas Convincingly

Your idea might be brilliant. Sharp, efficient, game-changing even. But if you can't pitch it in a way that lands, on the first try, in the first meeting, without losing your audience, you'll watch it die on the conference room table.

Welcome to the underappreciated art of convincing communication.

Convincing isn't manipulation. It's not trickery. It's the disciplined skill of framing your idea so it makes sense in someone else's brain, not just yours. That means clarity. Structure. Strategic empathy. And above all, restraint.

Let's start with the fundamentals.

Clarity Is Not Simplicity

Many professionals think clarity means "dumb it down." It doesn't. It means removing friction. Complexity is fine, if it's clean. If your listener has to wade through six metaphors, a back-story, and two disclaimers to understand your point, you've lost them.

Clarity starts with what you need to understand: your core message. If you can't summarize your idea in a single sentence, one that doesn't rely on jargon, you haven't clarified it for yourself yet.

Ask yourself:

- What do I want them to understand?

- Why does it matter to them?

- What do I want them to do next?

If you can't answer those in under 30 seconds, don't present. Rewrite. Reframe. Then speak.

Build in a Logical Arc

Even in fast-paced settings, your idea needs a skeleton. Start with the "why", not your bio, not the origin story of the proposal, not a trend quote from Harvard Business Review. Open with stakes:

- What problem are we solving?

- Why does it matter now?

- What's the cost of inaction?

Once you've established relevance, then you present the idea. One sentence. Then two supporting points. Then a quick preview of impact.

This isn't just good structure. It mirrors how human attention works. We pay attention to threats and opportunities first. Then we want the map. Only after that do we start evaluating the details.

Most bad presentations fail because they reverse this order. They start with features instead of problems, benefits before barriers, and overload before relevance. Don't do that.

Know Your Audience's Motivators

Professionals often present based on what they find exciting. They emphasize innovation, values, or efficiency. But what does your audience value?

A director of operations may care more about cost and feasibility than vision. A head of marketing may want differentiation, not just delivery. Your job isn't to force enthusiasm, it's to translate your idea into their priorities.

This doesn't mean pandering. It means fluency.

To present convincingly, you must speak the dialect of their decision-making. Match their pace. Anticipate objections. Use language they recognize as practical, not aspirational.

One trick: before any pitch, ask yourself what keeps your audience up at night. If your idea doesn't touch that pain point, it won't land.

Visuals Aren't a Crutch, They're a Shortcut

There's a reason good slides work: the brain processes visuals faster than language. But bad slides are worse than no slides. They interrupt flow, confuse context, and make you look like you're compensating.

Use visuals as clarity devices, not decoration. One chart that shows before-and-after outcomes. One image that maps the ecosystem you're addressing. One diagram that frames the problem space.

If you need more than three slides to make a point, your message isn't ready. Simplify the idea first.

Language Matters More Than You Think

Avoid qualifiers. Avoid fillers. Avoid anything that sounds like you're trying to get permission to speak.

Do not say:

- *"I think maybe this could work..."*

- *"This might be a little out there, but..."*

- *"I know this is probably obvious, but..."*

Conviction is contagious. So is self-doubt.

Instead, speak in declarative statements:

- *"This approach reduces cost by 17% in our pilot model."*

- *"Here's why this is worth exploring now."*

- *"We have a narrow window of opportunity, and this strategy positions us to act."*

This isn't arrogance. It's clarity wrapped in momentum.

Handle Pushback Without Losing the Room

The best presenters don't just prepare their points. They prepare for resistance.

You don't have to win every objection on the spot. But you do need to show that you anticipated it. *"That's a fair concern, here's how we're addressing it."* Or, *"We're running additional tests to confirm that, but the early data supports our direction."*

If someone derails your presentation with a loaded question or cynical comment, don't match tone. Reframe. Anchor back to the problem you're solving. Keep gravity in your voice, not defensiveness.

And if you don't know? Say so. But give a timeline for when you will. Confidence and transparency are not opposites.

The Final 10 Seconds: Stick the Landing

Most professionals end weak. They trail off into Q&A, throw in a vague "so yeah, that's the idea," or end on an awkward laugh.

Instead, end with clarity and force. Reassert your message. Restate your outcome. Issue a next step. Even if the next step is just reflection.

Examples:

"That's the idea. It cuts waste, speeds up turnaround, and works with what we already have. I'd love your initial thoughts."

"I'll send a one-page summary after this, but if you're aligned, we're ready to prototype next week."

Leave the room knowing what you want, and what you want from them.

If you can make your point fast, frame it in their language, and hold your ground under pressure, you don't need charisma. You need readiness.

Building Persuasive Arguments with Emotional Appeal

Logic builds the ladder. Emotion climbs it.

You can have the cleanest argument in the room, tight logic, bulletproof stats, airtight flow, but if nobody feels it, nobody moves. That's the core principle of persuasion: we don't act because something makes sense. We act because something makes meaning.

This section breaks down how to use emotion, not as manipulation, not as noise, but as an amplifier for truth. When done well, emotional appeal doesn't undercut logic. It completes it.

Start with Empathy, Not Ego

The most persuasive arguments don't start with *"what I want you to understand."* They start with *"what you're already feeling but haven't named yet."*

If your audience is anxious, acknowledge that.

If they're skeptical, respect it.

If they're excited but stuck, mirror that energy.

You're not softening the pitch, you're syncing with their emotional frequency. Empathy isn't about agreeing with everything. It's about demonstrating that you get where they're standing before asking them to walk somewhere new.

Try:

- *"I know this sounds like another initiative fighting for time and budget. That's fair. But here's why this one clears a different bar."*

- *"A lot of us are tired of ideas that sound good in theory but die in execution. This is built for traction, not theater."*

You're not soothing. You're grounding.

Anchor in Shared Values

Emotional appeal doesn't mean sentimentality. It means alignment. The question isn't *"how do I make this sound inspiring?"* It's *"how does this connect to what we already care about?"*

People move when something feels like a reflection of their identity or values. Tap that.

In professional settings, those values often include:

- Innovation with stability

- Team wellbeing

- Mission impact

- Autonomy and trust

- Long-term value over short-term flash

Your job is to thread the needle between your idea and one of these drivers.

Example:

"We've always said we want to lead, not follow. But right now, we're reacting. This idea puts us back in control, measurably, and fast."

"If we say we care about team sustainability, this is how we back it up with systems, not speeches."

This is how emotion becomes fuel, not fluff.

Use Narrative as Emotional Architecture

When data fails, stories work.

You don't need a full origin myth. Just a snapshot that puts human stakes into play.

If your argument is abstract, bring in a name.

If your point is strategic, bring in a moment.

If your logic is clean but cold, warm it with a face.

Instead of: *"Surveys show a 42% drop in engagement."*

Say: *"Last week, we lost a talented developer, not because of money, but because they felt invisible. That loss isn't rare. It's a symptom."*

A story is not a detour. It's the on-ramp.

Just don't overdo it. Emotional appeal collapses when it feels forced, manipulative, or irrelevant. You're not writing a novel. You're offering a human lens.

Show Stakes, Not Just Benefits

People don't act for abstract wins. They act to avoid real losses, or to chase something they already fear slipping away.

Instead of listing benefits, highlight stakes. What happens if we don't act? What's already being lost?

This doesn't mean fear-mongering. It means clarity.

"If we keep rotating vendors every quarter, we don't just waste money. We kill momentum."

"If we delay another month, we lose not just opportunity, but credibility."

Then you pivot: *"Here's how we stop the bleed."*

Emotion is high-octane when tied to consequence.

Let Your Own Conviction Show, But Stay Measured

Professionals often suppress passion, thinking it looks unprofessional. That's a mistake.

Flatness kills credibility just as fast as overacting.

Let your voice carry urgency. Let your face reflect belief. Just don't beg. Don't oversell. Don't corner people emotionally into agreement.

The rule is simple: express conviction like someone who respects disagreement.

If you find yourself trying to impress the room, pull back. If you find yourself trying to serve the room, move forward.

Your emotion should be rooted, not reactive.

Invite Action That Resonates, Not Just Instructs

You've made your case. You've tapped the values. Now what?

Don't end with *"any questions?"*

End with direction that feels like the next step. Emotional appeal is about more than agreement, it's about momentum.

Try:

- *"If this speaks to where we're stuck, let's test it in a live case this month."*

- *"If we're aligned, I'd like your blessing to run this quietly on one team and report back."*

Make the action low-bar, high-value, and emotionally frictionless.

In the end, emotional appeal is not about drama. It's about direction. You're not just telling people what to think, you're helping them feel why it matters.

Storytelling as a Tool for Effective Communication

If facts are the bricks, story is the mortar. It's what holds attention together. What makes abstract data human. What turns a list of features into a reason to care.

In business, story isn't optional anymore. It's not a "creative" bonus, it's the delivery system for every idea worth listening to. And it's your secret weapon if you're trying to cut through noise without shouting.

Let's break down how to use it well.

Start with the Point, Not the Plot

Most people think a story needs suspense. It doesn't. Not in the workplace. Your audience isn't looking to be entertained, they're looking to understand. Fast.

So before you launch into a story, make sure you've earned the space for it. That means previewing the point. Framing the why.

Instead of:

- *"Back in 2018, I was working with this startup, let me tell you what happened."*

Try:

- *"This story shows why moving fast without a system back-fires. Here's what happened."*

Now you've invited attention with purpose. They're listening for insight, not just anecdotes.

Choose the Right Type of Story

Every story you tell should fall into one of four buckets:

- **Origin Story** – How something began. Use this to explain culture, motivation, or strategy.

- **Conflict Story** – A problem that required a tough decision. Use this to demonstrate judgment.

- **Transformation Story** – A before-and-after moment. Use this to highlight impact.

- **Warning Story** – A cautionary tale. Use this to explain risk without being abstract.

The key is intentionality. If your story doesn't serve the idea, scrap it. Even a good story wastes time if it dilutes the message.

Keep It Short, Specific, and Unpolished

The most powerful workplace stories don't sound like TED Talks. They sound like moments, messy, fast, unfinished. Let them be real.

Cut out everything that doesn't build tension or clarify stakes.

Instead of:

- *"It was a Tuesday morning, I think around 9:30 or so..."*

Say:

- *"We'd just lost a contract, morale was wrecked, and our lead engineer said what everyone else was too scared to."*

Keep your pacing tight. Keep names and roles minimal. You're not building a world. You're highlighting a moment of friction, change, or insight. Then you land the point.

If you're telling the story well, no one's going to miss the fluff you cut.

Use Story to Teach, Not Just Tell

Good storytelling in communication doesn't just "share an experience." It invites reflection.

You're not trying to impress people with what you learned. You're giving them something to take away.

After you tell a story, ask a question. Frame a choice. Contrast what happened with what could have happened.

"What would've happened if we hadn't paused that launch?"

"Most teams would've walked away at that point. What kept us in it?"

"The lesson wasn't in the mistake, it was in how we responded. What would we change now?"

This turns story into engagement. And engagement into insight.

Match Tone to Audience

You can be funny. You can be raw. You can even be vulnerable, if you know your audience.

The mistake most professionals make isn't being too formal. It's being too self-referential. They try to make themselves the hero of the story instead of the conduit for meaning.

Here's the test: if your story makes you look too good, it's probably the wrong story.

Try stories where you made a hard call, took a risk, or admitted a blind spot. Show growth. Show complexity. That's what people trust.

And always match the energy of the room. Don't bring a high-drama anecdote into a room full of data analysts. Don't bring dry operational stories into a creative brainstorm. Adjust your tempo, not just your words.

Don't Use Stories to Avoid Saying the Hard Thing

There's a difference between using stories to illuminate, and using them to dodge.

If your idea requires a tough ask, don't hide it behind a story. Lead with the ask. Then give the story that shows why it matters.

For example:

"We need to restructure the team, starting next week. Before I explain the logistics, here's the experience that shaped this call."

Reverse that order, and it sounds like a stall tactic. Use story to humanize decisions, not delay them.

Practice Out Loud, Not Just on Paper

Even the most well-written story can fall flat if your delivery is wooden or meandering. So practice. Not to memorize, but to get the feel right.

Record yourself. Time it. Watch for filler words. Sharpen the transitions.

If you get bored telling your own story, cut it in half.

And if you're telling the same story repeatedly? Update the framing. Give it fresh stakes. Make it feel present, not recycled.

A story well told doesn't just inform, it moves. If you can take your idea and wrap it in human stakes, lived insight, and sharp delivery, you won't just be heard. You'll be remembered.

Techniques for Overcoming Communication Barriers

Communication isn't broken because people aren't talking. It's broken because no one's listening, adjusting, or owning the friction. In most environments, especially fast-moving, politically loaded, or remote-first workplaces, miscommunication isn't the exception. It's the norm.

If you want to be the one who cuts through noise, resolves confusion, and actually gets things done, you need to know what breaks communication, and what fixes it in real time.

Here's how to spot the barriers, dismantle them fast, and keep conversations functional when tensions rise.

Barrier #1: Assumed Understanding

"I thought you meant..." is the postmortem phrase of countless failed projects.

We assume alignment because we're moving fast. We skip clarification because it feels redundant. And we default to shorthand, internal metaphors, or team lingo without checking if everyone shares the reference point.

Solution: Make confirmation a habit, not a performance.

Try:

"Let me replay what I heard to make sure I'm tracking."

"Here's what I'm taking away. If I've missed something, jump in."

This isn't overkill, it's leadership. Clarifying saves ten times more time than redoing misaligned work.

And when you're the one giving instructions? Ask, "What part sounds unclear or incomplete?" instead of "Does that make sense?" The latter invites politeness. The former invites truth.

Barrier #2: Mismatch Between Medium and Message

Text isn't always the right tool. Neither is a meeting. Neither is Slack, or Zoom, or a five-page memo. Communication collapses when the format doesn't match the weight, or ambiguity, of the message.

Sensitive issues need tone. Complex issues need diagrams. Fast changes need direct signals. Misalignment here is how trust erodes and confusion spreads.

Solution: Choose format by function.

- If it's emotionally charged, talk live or record a voice note.

- If it's process-heavy, build a visual (flowchart, timeline, table).

- If it's strategic, write it down with context and send in advance.

- If it's personal feedback, never type it out cold. Frame it live.

Don't just ask *"What's easiest?"* Ask "What gives this message the best chance of being understood as intended?"

That's your channel.

Barrier #3: Power Dynamics and Psychological Safety

Not everyone feels safe speaking up, even when you ask. Especially when feedback might contradict a superior, or when there's a known history of pushback, ridicule, or punishment.

Silence isn't agreement. It's survival.

Solution: Create feedback space that doesn't depend on performance.

Start with how you ask. Instead of "Any feedback?" try:

- *"What feels like the biggest blind spot here?"*

- *"Where could this break down in real use?"*

- *"What would you push back on if you didn't have to filter?"*

Then shut up and wait. Let the silence breathe. Watch who speaks and who scans the room for permission.

If you're the junior person in the room, reframe your question as curiosity, not critique:

"Can I ask how you landed on that choice? I want to understand the thought process better."

That slight shift can disarm defensiveness and open the door.

Barrier #4: Language That Triggers Defensiveness

The fastest way to tank a conversation? Frame your point like a personal attack. Even if your intent is neutral, the wrong phrasing can make someone dig in, shut down, or escalate.

Common triggers:

- *"You always..." / "You never..."*

- *"That doesn't make any sense."*

- *"I don't get why you'd think that."*

Solution: Focus on impact, not accusation.

Say:

- *"Here's what I noticed, and the impact I saw."*

- *"I might be missing something, but this raised a flag for me."*

- *"Help me understand the reasoning behind this piece. It's not connecting yet on my end."*

You're not sugarcoating. You're reducing resistance so the actual point gets through.

This is especially critical in cross-functional or high-stakes settings where ego is already in the room. Give people a path to engage without shame.

Barrier #5: Cultural and Contextual Gaps

What feels clear to you might be loaded, or meaningless, to someone from a different background, department, or location. References, tone, and even pace of speech vary widely across cultures and contexts.

Solution: Default to clarity over cleverness.

If you're presenting to a global or cross-functional team:

- Avoid idioms, slang, and humor that depends on shared cultural knowledge.

- Break long sentences into simpler, punchier ones.

- Use visual anchors when possible, maps, charts, timelines, cause-effect diagrams.

And if you're confused by someone else's delivery, ask directly:

- *"Is there a story or context behind this approach I should know?"*

- *"How do you see this playing out from your side of things?"*

That moves the conversation toward understanding instead of assumptions.

Barrier #6: Emotional Reactivity

Even smart, grounded professionals shut down when triggered. Stress floods clarity. Pride overpowers logic. And suddenly, you're not debating a strategy, you're arguing to win.

Solution: Slow the tempo. Narrate the tension.

If things get heated:

- Call it in the room: *"I feel like we're escalating a bit, want to pause and reset?"*

- Reframe the goal: *"Let's remember what we're solving for. We're not on opposite sides of this."*

- Use body language intentionally, lower your voice, relax your shoulders, slow your speech.

- De-escalation isn't submission. It's leadership.

And if you're the one reacting? Say it out loud. *"I'm noticing I'm getting frustrated, and I want to stay constructive here. Give me a sec."* That kind of modeling gives permission for others to regulate too.

Communication isn't about avoiding conflict, it's about building enough skill and trust to move through it without losing your message.

Navigating Workplace Politics with Effective Communication

Workplace politics isn't always toxic. But it is always present.

Even in healthy organizations, power dynamics, informal alliances, and reputation games shape what gets heard, funded, or ignored. Communication in that environment isn't just about clarity, it's about strategy. You're not just speaking truth. You're speaking truth in a room that filters, edits, and remembers selectively.

Here's how to communicate with precision, protect your integrity, and still move the needle, even when the terrain isn't fair.

Understand the Real Audience

You're not always speaking to the people in the room. Sometimes you're speaking through them to someone else. Sometimes you're performing competence for future leverage. And sometimes you're speaking just enough to not be misquoted later.

That doesn't mean you're faking it. It means you're being aware of:

- Who's watching

- Who's repeating

- And who stands to gain or lose from your words

Before any big meeting, ask:

- What are the unspoken tensions here?

- Who's threatened by this idea?

- Who benefits if I succeed, or fail?

Then shape your delivery accordingly. Sometimes that means making someone else the messenger. Sometimes it means staying quiet until the room is ready. Other times it means speaking directly, but with layered framing that protects the idea from premature attack.

Make Others Feel Seen, Even When You Disagree

One of the fastest ways to tank your influence is to steamroll. Especially when power is uneven.

If someone you disagree with holds influence, formal or informal, your goal isn't to outmaneuver them in public. It's to build enough rapport that they don't automatically resist your ideas.

How?

- Validate their intention, even if you challenge their conclusion.

- Acknowledge their expertise before offering a different perspective.

- Ask for their take before proposing an alternative.

Examples:

- *"I can see where you're coming from, and I think that angle has real merit. There's another lens I'd love to add."*

- *"You've got more institutional memory on this than anyone. Can I offer a quick outside read on it?"*

This doesn't make you weak. It makes you hard to dismiss.

Don't Overshare Strategy, Protect Your Political Capital

In high-politics environments, transparency can backfire. Share too early, and your idea gets stolen. Share too much, and it gets picked apart before it can stand.

Instead:

- Share in layers.

- Give just enough to test interest, gauge alignment, and identify silent resistance.

- Save the details for when the room is safe, or the alliances are in place.

This isn't secrecy. It's pacing. Let your idea grow legs before it faces wind.

And if someone tries to corner you in public? Reframe the urgency.

- *"That's something I'm still shaping, happy to talk it through offline once I've vetted a few key pieces."*

- *"Let me tighten that before I float it too wide. Right now it's still exploratory."*

You're not evading. You're controlling narrative velocity.

Use Strategic Silence

Silence is a signal. It can be space for others to speak, or a boundary against pressure. In political environments, silence can also protect you.

Use it when:

- A decision hasn't been made, and you're being pressured to take a side.

- A rumor or narrative is circulating, and engaging would validate it.

- A superior is escalating emotionally, and you need to let the room breathe.

Strategic silence isn't withdrawal. It's pause-as-power.

But don't confuse it with passivity. When used intentionally, silence can amplify the moments you do choose to speak. It makes your words land harder, not weaker.

Frame Disagreement as Contribution, Not Combat

You don't win political battles by "calling people out." You win by making your input hard to reject.

This requires tone control. Curiosity framing. And language that turns confrontation into collaboration.

Try:

- *"Can I pressure test this idea with you?"*

- *"I want to see where this holds up under scrutiny, would you mind helping me sharpen it?"*

- *"We're probably seeing this from different sides, which is actually helpful here."*

The more you normalize disagreement without triggering turf war energy, the more influence you gain.

And the better you model this for others, the less combative your environment becomes over time.

Don't Assume Alignment Means Loyalty

Just because someone supports you in public doesn't mean they'll defend you in private. And just because they agree once doesn't mean they're bought in long-term.

This is where your communication shifts from reactive to relational.

Stay connected. Follow up. Credit others generously when things succeed. Ask for feedback even when you don't need it.

Why? Because people remember how you made them feel after the pitch. Your political capital is built in follow-up, not just delivery.

And if someone undercuts you later? Don't retaliate. Redirect:

"I might've misunderstood the earlier alignment, we can sync offline and clarify."

You're signaling boundaries without inviting war.

In political spaces, communication is less about brilliance and more about timing, tone, and trust. Play the long game. Let your ideas win on merit, but don't forget they need a map, a moment, and a messenger.

The Role of Emotional Intelligence in Team Communication

You can have the best systems, sharpest tools, and clearest strategy, but if your team can't talk to each other without triggering a breakdown, nothing works.

That's not a "culture" problem. It's an emotional intelligence problem.

Emotional intelligence (EQ) isn't just about being nice or emotionally expressive. It's about self-awareness, emotional regulation, and the ability to read the room without making it about you. In communication, EQ is the difference between teams that spiral under pressure and teams that stabilize each other when it hits.

Here's how EQ shapes, and saves, team communication.

Self-Awareness: Knowing What You Bring Into the Room

Every conversation starts before the first word. You bring your mood, your mental models, your baggage. So does everyone else.

If you're not aware of your own patterns, your tendency to dominate, withdraw, deflect, or rush, you'll default into them every time stress spikes. And so will the people around you.

Solution: Build the habit of naming your state before reacting.

Ask yourself:

- Am I defensive or open right now?

- Am I solving a problem or proving a point?

- Am I listening to respond or to understand?

This is internal hygiene. It doesn't require a performance, just enough awareness to keep your communication aligned with your actual goals, not your momentary ego.

And if you're off? Name it.

- *"I'm running hot right now, so let me slow down."*

- *"This hit a nerve, can we loop back in 10 minutes once I get clear?"*

That one pause can save an entire team spiral.

Self-Regulation: The Discipline Behind the Message

Team conflict isn't usually about the disagreement. It's about how that disagreement is handled. And that's where regulation kicks in.

You can't control what triggers you, but you can control what you do next.

That includes:

- Tone and tempo of your response

- Willingness to pause instead of escalate

- Choosing curiosity over correction when something lands wrong

Think of EQ as response architecture. It builds the container that allows the message to be received without defensive distortion.

Try:

- *"Let me step back and make sure I heard that right before I react."*

- *"Can I replay what I think you're saying? I might've read tone into it."*

This isn't about deference. It's about maintaining the clarity channel, even under stress.

Social Awareness: Reading the Room, Not Just the Words

The smartest teams don't just communicate well, they perceive well. They notice silence. They recognize tension. They hear the subtext.

If a teammate who normally contributes is quiet, it's not "nothing." It's a signal.

If someone agrees too quickly, it might be pressure, not alignment.

EQ-trained communicators don't steamroll past these signs. They slow down. They ask.

Examples:

- *"You've been a bit quiet, what's your take?"*

- *"I'm sensing some hesitation, want to talk it through before we commit?"*

Social awareness also means knowing when to speak to the room's energy, not just through it.

- *"Feels like we're all a little maxed out, should we step back and reassess before we force a decision?"*

- *"I know this issue's been polarizing. Let's name what's hard about it before we decide what's next."*

This makes teams feel seen. And people who feel seen communicate better, every time.

Empathy: Understanding Without Absorbing

Empathy isn't agreement. It's attunement.

You can fully disagree with a teammate's approach and still show that you understand how they got there.

When people feel understood, their nervous system relaxes. They become less rigid. More open. Which makes resolution possible.

Empathy phrases:

- *"I can see why you'd be frustrated. That makes sense given the timeline we gave."*

- *"That sounds like it put you in a tough spot. I hadn't thought about it from that angle."*

This isn't emotional labor. It's cognitive connection. You're not solving their feelings, you're holding space for their perspective so communication doesn't shut down under tension.

And if you're the one asking for empathy? Be clear:

- *"I don't need agreement. Just want to feel like my read isn't totally off base."*

That clarity invites compassion without demanding resolution.

Motivation: Using Shared Purpose to Refocus

When team communication stalls, it's often because the why has drifted.

Reminding people of shared purpose isn't corny, it's anchoring.

High-EQ communicators use motivation to re-center when the room gets fragmented:

- *"Can we remember what we're trying to protect here?"*

- *"We all want this to succeed, we just see different paths. Let's map both.”*

You're not overriding differences. You're rethreading the conversation to something larger than ego.

This is especially helpful in long projects, post-conflict debriefs, or high-fatigue cycles where people default into silos.

Repair: When EQ Means Owning the Miss

Even the most emotionally intelligent teams mess up. What separates them is the willingness to repair fast and directly.

Own your misreads.

- *"I missed your signal earlier. That's on me."*

- *"I overreacted yesterday. I want to fix that."*

And don't wait for a formal moment. EQ lives in small course corrections that accumulate over time.

When teammates model that kind of repair, psychological safety builds. Trust grows. And communication becomes more than functional, it becomes resilient.

Emotional intelligence isn't soft. It's the most durable edge in communication. It lets you lead without dominating, resolve without collapsing, and speak in a way people actually want to hear.

4

CREATIVE THINKING FOR UNIQUE SOLUTIONS

Techniques to Stimulate Creative Thinking

C reativity isn't a talent reserved for artists or visionaries, it's a tool. And like any tool, it can be sharpened, shaped, and wielded with intention. But in high-pressure work environments or fast-moving problem-solving sessions, most people default to the familiar. That's the enemy of innovation. You don't need to become a different person to think creatively. You just need to disrupt the ruts your brain naturally falls into.

Let's start with the obvious: if your solutions always look the same, your thinking process probably does too.

Technique 1: The Constraint Reversal

It sounds paradoxical, but creativity often thrives under restriction. In fact, when too many options are on the table, the brain flattens. It can't distinguish the bold from the feasible. That's where constraint reversal comes in.

Here's how it works: take one of your known limitations, budget, time, personnel, and flip it. If you normally ask, *"How do I solve this with only $5,000?"* ask instead, *"What would this look like if I had $5 million?"* Then, without dismissing any ideas, list solutions that emerge in that unconstrained state. Next, work backward. How could you simulate or approximate the high-budget version with what you do have?

Why this works: Constraint reversal lifts mental pressure, tricking the brain into thinking more freely. Then it forces you to translate ambition into practicality. It's not idealistic, it's iterative. The constraint still exists, but it stops being the starting point.

Technique 2: Cross-Context Substitution

One of the fastest ways to break conventional thought loops is to pull in frameworks from completely unrelated fields. If you're solving a supply chain issue, ask, *"How would a wedding planner handle this?"* If you're designing a digital product, *"What would a stage director do with this flow?"*

These substitutions don't have to make perfect sense. In fact, they shouldn't. The goal is to jolt your brain into new patterns by introducing unfamiliar analogies. A project manager I worked with restructured her client onboarding process after studying how theme parks manage crowd flow. She didn't copy the model, but she rethought touchpoints, expectations, and emotional pacing in a way that radically improved client retention.

Too often, people only look sideways, at competitors, or adjacent industries. Real creative breakthroughs come from looking diagonally, even absurdly.

Technique 3: Provocative Triggers

Edward de Bono called them "provocations", statements designed to be deliberately irrational or disruptive. Try this: *"Let's assume customers should never speak to us directly."* Or, *"What if we charged clients not to use our product?"*

Ridiculous? Exactly. The point is not to implement the provocation. It's to use it as a creative wedge. It pries open your assumptions.

You can generate these triggers by rewriting your problem statement in the most illogical or extreme way possible. Then explore: What is this showing me about my blind spots? It's often where the provocation feels most uncomfortable that the assumption is hiding.

Provocations aren't jokes, they're cognitive drills. Use them sparingly, but seriously.

Technique 4: The 30 Circles Challenge (Visual Divergence)

Sometimes language limits us. Especially in group settings, where people fear sounding weird or impractical. Visual tools bypass that hesitation.

The 30 Circles Challenge is simple: draw 30 blank circles on a page. Set a timer for 3 minutes. Your task is to turn as many circles into recognizable objects as possible. A sun. A clock. A cookie. A wheel. No repeats. No self-editing.

This isn't about art, it's about fluency. Most people start strong and stall out around 10–12. That's when the real creative stretch begins. You're forced to abandon common ideas and reach for unfamiliar ones.

Repeat this often, even in quiet moments. It trains your brain to resist premature closure, the tendency to jump on the first reasonable idea and stop exploring.

Technique 5: Obstacle Framing

Reframe your obstacle as the goal. If your team is burned out on performance metrics, ask, *"What if our goal was to intentionally underperform in Q3, but still retain customer loyalty?"* Suddenly, you're thinking about what makes customers stay when performance lags. What habits matter more than output? What non-metric elements build trust?

This isn't just reframing for fun. It's a practical tactic to escape problem exhaustion. When you're stuck solving the same issue with the same approach, flip the frame. Ask, *"What if failure is the goal?"* or *"How could this problem actually be an advantage?"* Then work from there.

Obstacle framing doesn't magically produce answers, but it forces attention toward what's been ignored. And in that ignored space, useful friction lives.

Technique 6: The SCAMPER Method (with a Twist)

SCAMPER, Substitute, Combine, Adapt, Modify, Put to another use, Eliminate, Reverse, is a staple in innovation workshops. But most people use it like a checklist. That's not creative thinking, it's mechanical brainstorming.

Here's the twist: pick one SCAMPER lens and apply it obsessively. For example, Eliminate. What can you remove from the process, product, or idea that would still deliver the core value? What if your service had no interface? No onboarding? No explanation?

Obsession leads to depth. And depth is where ideas stop being predictable.

SCAMPER works when it's used as a magnifying glass, not a microscope slide. Don't just apply it, challenge it.

None of these techniques work if you use them once and call it growth. Creativity isn't a breakthrough, it's a practice. Build a routine that includes at least one mental disruption per week. Juggle absurdity. Welcome discomfort. Make space for failure as a required ingredient.

Because the truth is, most creative blocks aren't a lack of ideas. They're a refusal to think past what feels efficient.

Let discomfort become the shortcut.

Using Mindfulness to Enhance Creativity

There's a reason your best ideas show up in the shower, or just as you're falling asleep. It's not magic. It's silence. It's the rare moment when your brain isn't being whipped around by competing priorities, social noise, or task-switching fatigue. That's where mindfulness comes in. It acts as a cognitive reset button.

For problem-solvers living in "go mode," mindfulness feels inefficient. But in reality, it's one of the fastest ways to access lateral thinking. It doesn't feed you ideas, but strips away the static that usually drowns them out.

Why Mindfulness Matters for Creative Thought

Creative thinking isn't just about generating ideas, it's about noticing them. And that noticing requires a certain mental stillness. When urgency, judgment, or internal commentary hijack your attention, your mind shifts into reactivity. Creativity shuts down. You default to familiar solutions, not because they work best, but because they shout the loudest.

Mindfulness interrupts that loop.

The practice doesn't demand detachment from the world. It demands presence within it. And presence is the condition under which creative inputs can actually register.

A Stanford study (Zeidan et al., 2010) found that even short bursts of focused attention training improved cognitive flexibility and working memory, two non-negotiables for innovation. Another (Colzato et al., 2012) linked open-monitoring meditation to increased idea generation across divergent thinking tasks. Translation: mindfulness makes your mind more spacious and less territorial.

Technique 1: Focused Attention Drills

This is the mental equivalent of sharpening a blade before you cut through cluttered thought. You don't need a mat or a mantra. Just a timer and a task.

Set 3–5 minutes. Focus on a single sensory input, your breath, the hum of a fan, the feel of your fingertips. Every time your attention drifts, pull it back with quiet insistence.

This drill isn't about relaxation. It's about control. You're training your brain to resist hijacking. Over time, this same muscle helps you hold multiple ideas in your mind without losing the thread. That's what complex creativity often demands.

In fast-moving industries, even five minutes of pre-meeting mindfulness can mean the difference between regurgitating old frameworks or offering something actually original.

Technique 2: Nonjudgmental Observation

Most people kill their ideas before they have a chance to walk. *"That's dumb." "That won't work." "That's not how we do things here."*

Mindfulness challenges that reflex. Instead of evaluating every mental output, you learn to observe. Let the thought pass. Let the idea exist without interrogation.

Try this: open a notes app or a physical notebook. Set a timer for 7 minutes. Write down every idea, phrase, image, or concept that enters your mind. No censoring. No editing. Don't aim for usefulness, aim for presence. Notice what shows up when you're not actively trying to be clever.

This is the entry point to raw ideation. Often, what feels useless at first will later become the seed of a breakthrough. But that only happens if you let it survive long enough to take root.

Technique 3: Environment Scanning

We're conditioned to overlook the familiar. That's why people walk past the same crooked painting for years and stop noticing it's tilted. Creativity dies in overfamiliarity.

Mindfulness, when applied externally, reactivates awareness. Try this exercise: for 10 minutes, walk through your home, office, or neighborhood without labeling anything. Don't say *"chair"* or *"tree"* in your mind, just observe. Note patterns, shadows, colors, angles. Try to see what you haven't seen in a while.

This isn't just visual play. It retrains your brain to spot novelty and detail. That same skill is transferable to problem environments. You start noticing friction points in your workflow because they're bent, off, or oddly consistent.

And from there, creativity follows curiosity.

Technique 4: The Mindful Pause

You don't need to be a monk to build creative reflexes. One of the most practical habits you can form is the pause.

Before responding. Before launching a new project. Before proposing your solution. Just pause.

Ask:

- *What am I reacting to?*

- *Is this thought a response, or a reflex?*

What would I notice if I waited 30 more seconds?

That pause doesn't delay progress, it sharpens it. Because the goal isn't speed. The goal is precision. A mind that rushes to solve often misses the real problem. A mind that pauses sees the edge.

This habit, if practiced deliberately, becomes a quiet power move. In meetings, it makes you unshakeable. In conflict, it makes you clear. And in creativity, it opens doors others didn't even know were there.

Letting Boredom Do Its Job

There's one more truth worth mentioning: most people treat boredom like a virus. Something to avoid, treat, escape. But boredom, in the right context, is a doorway.

When the brain isn't occupied, it starts making new connections. That's why some of your weirdest, smartest thoughts come when you're standing in line or staring at a ceiling. But modern life doesn't allow boredom anymore, we crush it with scrolling, snacking, multitasking.

So start practicing micro-boredom. Give yourself 5–10 minutes of intentional stillness. No podcast. No screen. No checklist. Just sit with yourself. Let the discomfort wash through. Your brain will fidget. Then it will wander. Then it will create.

Mindfulness isn't just a personal upgrade, it's a professional asset. It widens the margins of your mind so new ideas can enter. It tempers the rush to judgment so unusual solutions can emerge.

And perhaps most importantly, it makes room for you to access the one thing most problem-solvers forget to use: themselves.

You're not a creativity machine. You're a pattern-breaking human. Act like it.

Balancing Analytical and Creative Thought Processes

There's a reason "overthinking" is rarely a compliment. It signals paralysis, not clarity. But the opposite, wild, untethered ideation, can be equally unproductive. The real power lies in the blend. Creative solutions that survive the real world don't just emerge from daydreams; they're tested, refined, and made viable through structured analysis.

Most people treat analytical and creative thinking like opposites. They're not. They're partners. But like any pair, they need clear roles and good timing. When the roles blur, or the timing's off, the result is either chaos or stagnation.

Let's break down how to move between these two modes without short-circuiting either.

The Creative First, Analytical Second Rule

Creativity is fragile in the early stages. It dies fast when met with evaluation. That's why the order matters.

Step one: generate freely. Step two: analyze selectively.

Too many teams, and individuals, try to do both at once. They'll throw out an idea and immediately shoot it down: "That won't scale." "Legal won't approve it." "Nice, but the budget, "

This is like planting a seed and stepping on it before it sprouts. Let it grow first. Then test it.

Try this two-phase approach:

- **Phase 1:** Free Ideation (no filters, no criticism, just raw output)

- **Phase 2:** Strategic Evaluation (apply criteria like feasibility, scalability, impact)

You'll produce fewer safe ideas and more useful ones. Because creativity unshackled by logic is expansive, and logic applied to creativity makes it real.

Knowing Your Default Mode

Everyone leans one way. Some are idea generators, always chasing the novel. Others are practical skeptics, focused on risk, structure, and outcomes. Neither is wrong, but both are incomplete alone.

If you tend to jump straight to execution, pause. Ask, "Have I explored enough divergent possibilities?" If you live in the realm of possibilities, ask, "What would it take to turn one of these into an action plan?"

This self-awareness matters. Because balance isn't a personality trait. It's a habit of toggling between roles.

Use prompts to calibrate your balance:

- For analytical overthinkers: *"What if I had to pitch three bad ideas right now?"*

- For creative idealists: *"What's one constraint that would force this idea to mature?"*

The goal isn't to neutralize your strengths. It's to round out your blind spots.

Building in Time for Both Modes

In real-world work, deadlines compress thought. But trying to cram analytical and creative processing into the same window kills quality.

Instead, block your time accordingly. Even in short sprints:

Use the morning for idea play, when your mind is less rigid.

Save the afternoon for sorting, trimming, and questioning.

You're not just protecting your ideas, you're respecting the different operating systems in your brain. Creativity thrives in openness and rest. Analysis thrives in clarity and pressure.

If you're leading a team, make this structure visible. Let people know when it's time for expansion versus refinement. Muddled expectations lead to half-baked results and frustration.

Practice: Dual-Column Thinking

This simple tool helps balance both processes on the page. Take a blank sheet and draw a vertical line down the center. On the left, write down raw ideas, no filters, no judgments. On the right, respond analytically to each one.

Example:

- **Left (Creative):** *"What if we offered our service without a website?"*

- **Right (Analytical):** *"We'd need an alternative customer interface, possibly SMS or direct email. That narrows reach but deepens engagement."*

The goal isn't to kill ideas. It's to walk beside them.

Over time, this method builds your ability to keep both muscles engaged, without letting one dominate.

When to Let Logic Sit Down

There are moments when logic needs to take a back seat, especially in early brainstorming or when tackling novel problems.

Signs you're stifling creativity with over-analysis:

- Every idea gets a *"yes, but, "* response.

- Your brainstorming sessions feel dry, repetitive, or quiet.

- You're solving for safety, not originality.

In these moments, declare a logic timeout. Say it out loud if needed: *"For the next 15 minutes, no evaluation. Only ideas."*

It may feel awkward at first, especially in corporate cultures trained to seek ROI before possibility. But you'll be shocked at what emerges when the fear of judgment is temporarily removed.

Just make sure the logic comes back in. Otherwise, you'll have a folder full of concepts with no runway.

Signs You're Leaning Too Far Creative or Too Far Analytical

Use this gut-check list:

- Too creative, not enough logic: You have dozens of ideas, but no next steps. Feedback feels vague. Progress stalls.

- Too analytical, not enough creativity: You're repeating old frameworks. Solutions feel safe but uninspired. You're "optimizing" something that may need to be reimagined.

Balance means you produce both:

- Quantity and quality.

- Imagination and execution.

- Wild ideas and tested pathways.

It's not about compromise. It's about timing.

Creativity needs freedom. Analysis needs structure. Innovation needs both. But they cannot share the same seat at the same time. Build a workflow that lets each drive, then switch the wheel with intention.

If you want original solutions that actually work, think like a dreamer. Then edit like an engineer.

Overcoming Resistance to Change with Creative Solutions

Let's name the tension: most people want change, but they hate changing. It's not laziness, it's neurological. The human brain is wired for efficiency, and change is expensive. It burns mental energy. It creates uncertainty. It threatens identity. And that's why even brilliant problem-solvers get stuck recycling the same ideas, running the same meetings, applying the same tired frameworks that no longer move the needle.

Creativity isn't just about generating novel ideas, it's about neutralizing the internal sabotage that keeps you from applying them. If you want creative problem-solving that works, you have to learn how to outsmart your own resistance. Because the resistance is real. And it's not going anywhere.

The Real Root of Resistance: Loss Aversion, Not Laziness

At the core of most resistance is loss aversion, the psychological tendency to fear loss more than we value gain. It's not that your team doesn't want the new system. It's that they're afraid of what they'll lose if they adopt it: familiarity, comfort, competence, control.

Creative thinkers don't bulldoze that fear. They design with it.

Start here: don't pitch your new idea as "better." Pitch it as "safer to try." Make the shift small, the stakes reversible. If people believe they can test without committing, resistance drops by half. This is called **low-stakes prototyping**, a creative solution not for the problem itself, but for the pushback that kills momentum.

When people feel they have an escape hatch, they're more likely to enter the room.

Reframing Change as an Experiment

One of the simplest mindset shifts for overcoming resistance is to rebrand change. Don't call it an "initiative" or a "rollout." Call it a trial. A sprint. A question we're testing.

The language matters. "We're changing how we onboard clients" triggers defensiveness. But *"We're trying a two-week experiment to see if X method improves engagement"* creates curiosity.

Experiments lower the threat level. They also position failure as data, not defeat.

That's the creative move: shifting from declaration to exploration. It doesn't make the change less real, it just makes it feel less permanent. That's often enough to get people in the door.

The Creative Disruption Loop

Here's a three-part structure that helps rewire resistant patterns using creativity:

- Interrupt the Pattern

Identify one micro-behavior you want to shift (e.g., "Team always defaults to email over direct conversation."). Now insert a disruptive alternative that's low-risk and slightly weird. For example, *"For the next two days, we're using voice memos only."*

- Reflect and Reframe

After the disruption window, invite reflection. What felt easier? What felt awkward? What did we assume would go wrong that didn't?

- Choose a Keeper

Instead of declaring success or failure, select one element to keep, and one to kill. This prevents the binary all-or-nothing thinking that fuels resistance.

The creative disruption loop works because it respects friction. It expects discomfort. But it doesn't let that discomfort run the show.

Design for the Skeptic, Not the Enthusiast

When you're crafting a new process or solution, don't design for the people who are already on board. Design for the skeptic. The overworked analyst. The annoyed manager who's seen "innovation week" fail three times already.

Ask:

- What would make this feel less risky?

- What's the smallest version of this idea we could pilot in a single afternoon?

- How could we prove value in 15 minutes?

Creativity often fails not because the idea was wrong, but because the rollout didn't account for psychological friction. Build solutions with adoption in mind, not just brilliance.

If it doesn't feel easy to start, it probably won't.

Addressing the Identity Threat

For many professionals, especially high performers, adopting a new idea feels like admitting the old one was flawed. That hits the ego hard.

So take the blame off the person, and place it on the context.

Instead of saying, *"This new tool will fix what's broken,"* say, *"The environment's changed, our tools have to evolve with it."*

This subtle reframe protects identity. It makes people feel like they're adapting to reality, not abandoning competence. Creative thinkers don't just design clever systems, they design emotionally intelligent ones.

Creative Incentives: Make It Fun, Not Mandatory

Serious change doesn't have to come from serious tone. Sometimes, lightness works better.

Try gamifying the new process. Track experiments visually. Create a shared "failure trophy" that gets passed around for bold attempts that didn't work. Celebrate friction, not just resolution.

These aren't gimmicks. They're behavioral incentives that disrupt default resistance.

One team I worked with created a "Wild Idea Wall" in the break-room where anonymous post-it notes could pitch anything, no consequences. One of those ideas ended up becoming a product test that doubled conversions. It worked because it bypassed the usual filter of *"Will this make me look smart?"*

Creativity needs room to be bad first. If your culture doesn't allow for that, it will stay stuck, however smart your people are.

The enemy of change isn't ignorance. It's threat. Creative problem-solving doesn't just mean better ideas, it means safer containers. Lower the heat, reframe the risk, inject play, and prototype the pain points.

People don't resist change because they're irrational. They resist because they're human. Your job isn't to fight that. It's to out-create it.

Case Studies in Successful Creative Problem Solving

Creativity doesn't always come wrapped in lightbulb moments or innovation awards. Sometimes, it looks like duct tape. A sideways decision. A workaround that shouldn't have worked but did. These moments prove the value of creative problem-solving as survival, not performance.

Here are five real-world cases where unconventional thinking unlocked solutions. No jargon. No miracles. Just sharp people refusing to let the obvious be the only option.

1. The 404 Page That Saved Customer Support

A small SaaS startup noticed something odd: customers were submitting an unusually high volume of tickets about broken links, particularly within their product help center. Instead of fixing every link individually, which would have taken months, they did something else.

They rewrote their 404 page.

Instead of a generic "page not found," they turned it into a self-diagnostic tool:

- Offered three quick links to the most commonly requested resources.

- Included a "Was this what you were looking for?" button.

- Auto-generated a support ticket only if the customer still clicked "No."

Support tickets dropped by 27% within two weeks.

Why it worked: they stopped solving the problem symptom (broken links) and addressed the user behavior (confusion at the point of friction). That's creative thinking: diagnosing sideways.

2. The Coffee Shop That Banned Laptops (and Profits Rose)

In a quiet Portland neighborhood, a local café noticed their midday revenue was dipping, even though the shop was full. The problem? Solo customers camped out for hours with laptops, ordering one drink and occupying prime tables.

Instead of pushing for more sales, they pulled the plug. No laptops between 11am and 2pm. They posted it kindly, enforced it gently, and added more small two-top tables.

Foot traffic increased. So did food orders. Groups started meeting there again, midday became social.

This wasn't about punishing productivity. It was about reclaiming space for the original business model. The owners resisted the pressure to chase digital nomads and got creative about protecting physical community.

Sometimes the best solution is subtraction.

3. The Hospital That Used LEGO for Workflow Design

A Swedish hospital was redesigning its pediatric emergency wing. But traditional workflow diagrams weren't helping staff visualize traffic patterns or pain points.

So one nurse manager brought in LEGO bricks.

They recreated the entire floorplan on a large table. Color-coded teams, replicated patient paths, and role-played common emergencies. It revealed pinch points no one had noticed on paper, like a vital supply room that was technically central, but functionally blocked during rush hours.

Adjustments were made before construction began. Costs were cut. Response times improved after the remodel.

Lesson: Creativity isn't just about the final product, it's about the design process. And sometimes, using a child's toy beats adult software.

4. The Nonprofit That Changed Its Name to Get Unstuck

An education nonprofit in Chicago struggled for years to expand its outreach. Every rebranding effort failed. People confused them with a government program due to their dry, bureaucratic name: "Community Academic Support Services."

A junior staffer floated an idea at a team lunch: *What if we just called ourselves The Homework Club?*

They laughed. Then paused.

Three months later, they filed the paperwork. "The Homework Club" became their front-facing identity. The tone changed. Kids joined. Parents remembered the name. Funders liked the clarity.

Applications tripled.

The idea wasn't strategic, it was intuitive, plainspoken, and a little silly. But it worked because it solved the real problem: nobody knew what they did.

Creativity, in this case, was just brutal honesty with better branding.

5. The Engineer Who Used Silence to Fix the Machine

At a mid-sized manufacturing plant in Ohio, a production line kept jamming every morning. Engineers ran diagnostics. Mechanics replaced parts. Nothing fixed it.

One technician decided to show up at 4 a.m., two hours before the jam usually started. He walked the floor and just listened. No tools. No testing.

After 30 minutes, he heard it: a low rhythmic clink near the cooling system, barely audible during regular hours. It turned out a single worn component was vibrating out of alignment as the ambient temperature rose.

They fixed the part. The jamming stopped. Downtime dropped by 38%.

What unlocked the solution? Not more tech. Not more staff. Just intentional silence. A deliberate pause in the noise.

That's what creative problem-solving often looks like: slowing down when everything tells you to speed up.

These stories have nothing in common on the surface, different industries, tools, and contexts. But the pattern is clear:

Each solution bypassed the obvious.

Each required a willingness to see the actual problem, not just the one that made the most noise.

Each trusted simplicity over sophistication.

Creative problem-solving isn't just about cleverness. It's about choosing to see what others ignore. Sometimes that means breaking a pattern. Sometimes it means naming the real problem with painful clarity. Sometimes it just means listening better.

But always, it means moving beyond default settings.

Brainstorming Beyond Boundaries: Innovative Approaches

Most brainstorming sessions fail because the structure punishes creative effort instead of supporting it. You get the same five voices dominating the room. The same sticky notes repeating last quarter's ideas. The same awkward pause after someone says, *"Let's think outside the box,"* as if the phrase itself is a substitute for actually doing it.

You don't need better thinkers. You need better conditions. Here's how to build a brainstorming system that does what it claims, pushes boundaries, surfaces originality, and breaks past the same recycled scripts.

Rule 1: Separate Generation from Evaluation

The fastest way to kill bold ideas is to evaluate them in real-time. That's not brainstorming, that's filtering. And it's why teams start safe and end stale.

Instead, use the double session rule:

- Session One is for volume. You're not allowed to discuss, judge, or rank anything.

- Session Two, held later, is for sorting, grouping, and pressure-testing.

That temporal separation lets novelty breathe. It also gives introverted or reflective thinkers time to contribute meaningfully.

If your team pushes back, remind them: bad ideas are raw material. Judging too early is like editing a sentence before it's written.

Rule 2: Use Unconventional Prompts

Most people brainstorm solutions. Try brainstorming problems instead.

Flip the prompt:

- *"What's a problem we've been avoiding?"*

- *"What's a problem we wish we had?"*

- *"What would break if we 10x'd this idea?"*

This pushes the group into second-order thinking, exploring implications, not just options. It also reveals blind spots and tension points that traditional prompts miss.

Another approach: use imagery or sound. Play an abstract soundscape and ask, *"What kind of product or system does this remind you of?"* Show a bizarre photo and ask, *"What story could this image be hiding?"*

These aren't gimmicks. They short-circuit cognitive rigidity. The brain gets bored of verbal logic. Surprise it with metaphor, color, absurdity. Then harness the chaos.

Rule 3: Invite Outsiders to Shake the Frame

Bring in someone who doesn't work on the problem. A customer. A junior staffer. A friend from another department. Their role isn't to give expert advice, but to ask untrained questions.

Outsiders don't carry the same assumptions. They haven't internalized what's "realistic." And that makes them valuable. Even if their questions are naive, they force reframing.

One finance firm brought in a theater director during a systems re-design session. He asked: *"Where's the stage? Who's your audience? What's the climax?"* At first, the team laughed. But the exercise shifted how they saw user interaction, leading to a redesigned interface that actually flowed like a performance, not a spreadsheet.

The best ideas often start from the worst questions. Especially when they come from someone who's not trying to impress.

Rule 4: Use Anonymous Submission, Then Reveal

Psychological safety is everything in brainstorming. But even "safe" environments come with invisible social pressure, hierarchy, identity, fear of being labeled impractical or odd.

One workaround: run the first idea round anonymously. Use digital tools (Google Forms, virtual sticky boards) to collect ideas without names. Then reveal and discuss only once the field is rich.

This shifts the power dynamic. It also tends to elevate underheard voices, often the quiet analyst, the junior staffer, the intern who's seen the problem but hasn't felt permission to say it out loud.

Once the floor is open, you'll find more engagement across the board. The group isn't protecting its image. It's protecting the process.

Rule 5: Set Artificial Constraints

Unlimited brainstorming sounds good on paper. In practice, it creates diffusion. Creativity feeds on pressure.

Try these constraint prompts:

- *"You can only use two colors, one material, and no screen."*

- *"You must design this in 24 hours with no budget."*

- *"Your idea must exclude our current customer base."*

These constraints sound ridiculous, but that's the point. They force lateral movement. They strip the safe ideas from your brain and demand new ones.

Don't aim for feasibility in this stage. Aim for stretch. You can always walk it back. But most groups never stretch far enough to need to.

Rule 6: End with Commitment, Not Consensus

Brainstorming without follow-through is just a creativity exercise. It burns time and morale.

The final five minutes should be brutal and clear:

- *"What's the most interesting idea that emerged?"*

- *"What's one experiment we'll test in the next 7 days?"*

- *"Who owns next steps?"*

You're not voting. You're picking. And that's the difference between imagination and traction.

The goal isn't to make everyone agree, it's to make one thing move.

Innovation isn't born in silence or chaos. It's born in structure, flexible enough to wander, solid enough to deliver. Good brainstorming honors both. It removes fear, inserts friction, and creates a temporary space where failure is allowed, weirdness is welcome, and usefulness is optional, until it isn't.

So if your next team meeting starts with *"Let's get creative,"* pause. Don't say it. Build it.

Make a Difference with Your Review

Unlock the Power of Sharing

"Be the reason someone believes in the goodness of people." — Unknown

Every action we take ripples outward, often in ways we can't predict. By leaving a review, you could be the spark that inspires someone to take charge of their critical thinking journey.

Are you ready to make that difference?

Why Your Review Matters

Picture someone standing where you once stood: eager to improve their decision-making, but unsure where to start. Your honest feedback might be the nudge they need to pick up *Think Sharp: How Anyone Can Master Critical Thinking and Problem-Solving for Smarter Decisions and Career Success.*

Here's the truth—most readers rely on reviews to decide which books are worth their time. And when you share your experience, you're not just helping me—you're helping someone just like you find the tools they need to succeed.

Your review could...

- Encourage a manager to lead their team more effectively.

- Inspire a career changer to take a bold leap forward.

- Equip a new graduate with the skills to excel in their first job.

- Give a lifelong learner the confidence to tackle new challenges.

How to Leave Your Review

It only takes a minute to make a lasting impact. Scan the QR code below or visit the link to share your thoughts:

https://www.amazon.com/review/review-your-purchases/?asin=B0F35WJHD8

Your support means the world to me. Thank you for being part of this journey to spread smarter decisions and brighter futures!

Warmly,

Renae C. Linde

5

Interactive Tools and Exercises

Practical Exercises for Cognitive Bias Recognition

You don't beat bias by wishing it away. You beat it by trapping it in the act.

Cognitive biases aren't flaws in character, they're patterns in processing. They save time, reduce complexity, and often work just fine. But in high-stakes decisions, they don't just skew the picture, they quietly redraw it. Recognizing bias, then, is about slowing down the reflex long enough to see the distortion before it sets the course.

Here are five practical, grounded exercises designed to help you recognize your own biases, not just understand them in theory, but catch them mid-thought when it counts.

1. The Confirmation Bias Inventory

Objective: Reveal how your search for evidence reinforces what you already believe.

Instructions:

- Pick one belief you hold with confidence, about a coworker, a political issue, or even your own strengths. Then:

- Search online or ask someone for a perspective that directly contradicts your belief.

- Write down three pieces of evidence supporting the opposing view.

- Without defending your original position, ask: *"If this were true, what would change about how I see this issue?"*

What it reveals: This exercise pulls your brain out of the echo chamber. You're not trying to change your mind, you're trying to see what your mind usually blocks.

2. The Assumption Audit

Objective: Surface the invisible assumptions driving your conclusions.

Instructions:

- Write down a recent decision or opinion you've formed (e.g., "That project is doomed").

- Ask: *"What must I believe to be true in order to think this?"*

- List at least three underlying assumptions.

- Then test: Are they facts, interpretations, or projections?

What it reveals: Most flawed decisions aren't based on bad logic, they're based on assumptions you didn't even realize you were making.

3. Bias Tagging in Real Time

Objective: Practice spotting bias as it happens in conversations.

Instructions:

- During your next team meeting or casual discussion, keep a running mental (or physical) log.

- Tag any statements that reflect potential biases:

  - Availability bias (*"That just happened last week, so it must be common"*)

  - Halo effect (*"He's great at presentations, he must be a good manager"*)

  - Sunk cost fallacy (*"We've already put too much time into this to quit now"*)

What it reveals: The real-time tagging turns abstract concepts into pattern recognition skills. You'll get better at hearing distortion in real conversations, including your own.

4. The Role Reversal Technique

Objective: Disrupt egocentric bias by adopting a different perspective.

Instructions:

- Think of a recent conflict, disagreement, or tension.

- Re-write the event from the other person's point of view as if they were completely rational and acting in good faith.

- Then ask: *"What does this version suggest I missed or misunderstood?"*

What it reveals: When you reframe the situation as though the other person isn't your enemy, you often find you've been reacting to a caricature, not a human. This breaks the feedback loop that reinforces your own righteousness.

5. The Pre-Mortem

Objective: Counteract optimism bias and planning fallacies by imagining failure first.

Instructions:

- Before starting a project or making a big decision, ask: *"It's six months from now. This failed. Why?"*

- Write down every reason you can think of, even unlikely or embarrassing ones.

- Now reverse-engineer safeguards based on what you just identified.

What it reveals: Your brain doesn't like imagining failure, but that's exactly why it matters. This exercise primes your critical faculties when they're most needed: before momentum and excitement take over.

These aren't magic tricks. They're friction points. Each exercise creates just enough pause to challenge your default pathways. And that's the goal, not to eliminate bias altogether, but to notice its pull and choose your response instead of reacting blindly.

Because the biggest problem with bias isn't that we have it.

It's that we believe we don't.

Interactive Quizzes to Strengthen Critical Thinking

The best quizzes don't just tell you what you know, they reveal how you think.

In a world stuffed with static assessments and personality-type labels, it's easy to forget that the real point of self-evaluation isn't classification. It's calibration. You don't take a critical thinking quiz to feel smart. You take it to expose where your reasoning breaks down, especially when it feels strongest.

Below are five interactive quiz structures. Each one sharpens a different mental edge, bias detection, logical clarity, emotional balance, ambiguity tolerance, and inference accuracy. You can try them yourself or adapt them for team workshops, mentoring sessions, or even hiring processes.

1. "What's the Flaw?" Challenge

Purpose: Identify logical fallacies in real-world statements.

How It Works:

- Present a list of 10–15 quotes or arguments pulled from debates, op-eds, or social media.

- For each one, the participant selects the type of fallacy committed:

  - Ad hominem

  - False dilemma

  - Slippery slope

  - Straw man

  - Appeal to authority

  - Circular reasoning

- Provide immediate feedback with explanations, not just correct answers but why the flaw matters in context.

Why It Works: It trains pattern recognition and builds a mental library of common reasoning traps that often go unnoticed in everyday language.

2. Bias Pairing Quiz

Purpose: Help users match scenarios to specific cognitive biases.

How It Works:

- Show a short scenario:

    - *"After reading several news stories about plane crashes, Jamie decides to drive on her next trip."*

- Present 3–4 possible biases:

    - Availability bias

    - Status quo bias

    - Overconfidence effect

- The user selects one and gets detailed feedback about why it fits (or doesn't).

Why It Works: This method forces nuance. Many situations involve more than one bias, but the quiz emphasizes primary drivers and encourages users to reflect on their own default assumptions.

3. Inference Builder

Purpose: Strengthen the ability to draw valid conclusions from incomplete or ambiguous data.

How It Works:

- Give a series of short "If... then..." premises, some with missing information.

- Ask: *"What conclusion can reasonably be drawn?"*

Example:

- If all B are C, and some A are B, then...?

- Choices: Some A are C / All A are C / Some C are A / Cannot be determined

Why It Works: Forces users to work within logical constraints, resisting the urge to "fill in" missing information based on instinct.

4. Emotion vs. Logic Sorter

Purpose: Build metacognitive awareness about how emotions color interpretation.

How It Works:

- Present real-life dilemmas or excerpts from decision-making situations.

- Ask users to score each option or reaction on a sliding scale from 1 (purely emotional) to 10 (purely rational).

- Follow with a reflective prompt: *"What made this response feel rational, and what emotional values might be embedded underneath?"*

Why It Works: It teaches people that rationality and emotion aren't opposites, they're layered. The goal isn't to eliminate feeling, but to disentangle it from reasoning when stakes are high.

5. The Ambiguity Tolerance Quiz

Purpose: Gauge and expand comfort with uncertain or conflicting information.

How It Works:

- Ask participants to read three complex scenarios involving moral gray areas, incomplete data, or open-ended outcomes.

- For each, ask:

  - What is the most reasonable decision?

  - What additional information would change your mind?

  - How comfortable are you with making a choice without full certainty? (Rate 1–10)

Why It Works: It surfaces discomfort people may not know they have with ambiguity and gives them a structured way to reflect on how they navigate uncertainty.

Each of these quizzes does more than test, it trains. They reinforce the muscle of pause, the reflex of second-guessing your first impression, and the habit of asking *"What am I missing?"* rather than *"Am I right?"*

You don't need to score 100% to win at critical thinking. You need to stay curious about why you didn't.

Digital Tools for Tracking Problem-Solving Progress

Progress isn't always visible. That's why tracking matters.

We tend to assume that good decisions should feel good. That clarity will arrive like a spotlight. That insight comes in neat bursts of brilliance. But real problem-solving is messy. Progress hides in drafts, reversals, and small pivots that don't feel productive in the moment. That's where digital tools come in, not to replace thinking, but to make its trajectory visible.

Below are five categories of tools that help structure, document, and reflect on your problem-solving process. You don't need to use all of them. But if you've ever walked away from a project unsure what you actually did, these can help.

1. Digital Whiteboards for Mapping Thought Flow

Recommended Tools: Miro, Lucidspark, Whimsical

Best Use: Visualizing relationships between ideas, people, or priorities.

Why It Works: When you're stuck in complexity, seeing the architecture of your thinking matters. Digital whiteboards let you drag, drop, and link pieces of a problem spatially, not just linearly. This encourages lateral thinking and pattern discovery, especially useful during brainstorming or systems mapping.

Pro Tip: Use color coding to track emotional charge (e.g., red = assumptions, green = verified data, yellow = unknowns). This builds awareness of how emotion and information intersect in your reasoning.

2. Progress Journals with Tags and Filters

Recommended Tools: Notion, Roam Research, Obsidian

Best Use: Capturing evolving thoughts, documenting decisions, and revisiting shifts over time.

Why It Works: A progress journal is more than a diary. It's a record of how your thinking matures. When you tag entries by topic, emotion, or outcome, you create searchable breadcrumbs. This makes it easier to detect decision patterns and adjust course in future projects.

Pro Tip: End each entry with two prompts:

- *"What did I assume today that might not hold?"*

- *"What changed in how I see the problem?"*

3. Decision Trackers with Outcome Reviews

Recommended Tools: Airtable, Trello, Asana with custom fields

Best Use: Structuring decision-making and tracking consequences over time.

Why It Works: We tend to remember decisions in isolation, not systems. A decision tracker creates a living document of the "why," not just the "what." You log the context, reasoning, emotional state, alternatives considered, and the eventual result. That post-decision review becomes a feedback loop for improving future judgment.

Pro Tip: Schedule a recurring reminder to revisit each major decision 30–90 days later and tag it as:

- Outcome better than expected

- Outcome worse than expected

- Unexpected outcome (neither good nor bad)

- Outcome still unfolding

4. Collaboration Platforms for Shared Problem Solving

Recommended Tools: Slack, Microsoft Teams, Google Workspace, ClickUp

Best Use: Group thinking, shared visibility, asynchronous brainstorming.

Why It Works: When problems cross roles or disciplines, collaboration platforms keep decision threads alive. Tools like threaded comments, polls, or document histories create a transparent ecosystem where assumptions are surfaced, challenged, and revised, not buried in someone's inbox.

Pro Tip: Designate a "Bias Breaker" on each project, someone assigned to raise contrarian points or play devil's advocate using a defined checklist. Rotate the role weekly to normalize cognitive friction.

5. AI-Powered Assistants for Meta-Reflection

Recommended Tools: ChatGPT, Mem, Reflect.app

Best Use: Challenging your thinking, rephrasing assumptions, or summarizing complexity.

Why It Works: AI tools won't replace critical thinking, but they can serve as mirrors. Ask them to summarize your argument, highlight logical gaps, or suggest opposing viewpoints. When used with intention, they accelerate mental clarity by pushing you beyond your defaults.

Pro Tip: Paste your own problem explanation into an AI prompt and ask: *"What assumptions am I making here?"* or *"What would someone with a different value system conclude?"*

These tools aren't about being more productive. They're about being more conscious. Conscious of how a decision evolved, where your blind spots emerged, and how your strategy changed under stress. That's what makes thinking traceable, and growth repeatable.

You don't need perfect systems. You need visible progress. And the best digital tools don't just capture what you did, they help you see how you think.

Using Games to Enhance Problem-Solving Skills

If you want to understand how someone thinks under pressure, don't give them a test. Give them a game.

Games reveal more than strategy, they expose temperament. How someone handles rules, adapts under constraint, weighs risk, and recovers from setbacks. And for those trying to sharpen their own thinking, games offer a rare kind of feedback: immediate, emotional, and embodied. You feel the consequence of a bad assumption. You notice when you relied too much on instinct.

Let's be clear, this isn't about gamification as a buzzword. It's about leveraging the actual structure of games to build mental flexibility, critical analysis, and pattern recognition. Here's how.

1. Deduction Games for Logical Precision

Examples: Codenames, Clue, The Resistance, Decrypto

Skill Target: Inference, elimination, reading between the lines.

Why It Works: Deduction games force you to work with limited, often ambiguous information. They demand that you form conclusions under uncertainty while avoiding overconfidence. In team-based deduction games, you also learn how poor communication and assumption bias derail strategy.

Try This Twist: After each round, debrief:

- What was your key assumption?

- What did you ignore that turned out to matter?

- Where did your reasoning break down?

2. Strategy Games for Systems Thinking

Examples: Settlers of Catan, Risk, Terraforming Mars, Wingspan

Skill Target: Long-term planning, resource allocation, adaptability.

Why It Works: Good strategy games are a sandbox for complex problem-solving. You have multiple inputs (resources, objectives, constraints), and the game rewards iterative planning. They simulate real-world tradeoffs: sacrifice now for advantage later? Collaborate or compete? Stick with the plan or pivot?

Solo Application: After playing, create a short write-up of your strategy and decision map. Revisit it after a few sessions to track how your patterns evolve.

3. Time-Pressure Games for Fast Thinking and Flexibility

Examples: Escape Room in a Box, Keep Talking and Nobody Explodes, 5-Minute Dungeon

Skill Target: Rapid prioritization, teamwork under pressure, thinking on your feet.

Why It Works: When you don't have time to second-guess, you discover what mental models you actually use. These games strip away posturing and perfectionism. What's left is reflex, raw, real, and incredibly instructive.

Debrief Prompt: *"What did we default to when time ran out, and did it help or hurt?"*

4. Open-Ended Games for Creative Divergence

Examples: Dixit, Rory's Story Cubes, What Do You Meme?, improv-based word games

Skill Target: Idea generation, analogical thinking, lateral creativity.

Why It Works: These games stretch your mind by disrupting predictable associations. They encourage metaphor, irony, misdirection, and playful risk. The goal isn't accuracy, it's originality. And that builds the kind of cognitive agility needed to reframe problems in real life.

Group Exercise: Use these as warm-ups before brainstorming sessions to loosen mental rigidity and open divergent channels.

5. Simulation and Roleplay Games for Perspective-Taking

Examples: Dungeons & Dragons, Fiasco, serious games used in business or social impact simulations

Skill Target: Empathy, scenario planning, behavioral analysis.

Why It Works: Roleplay forces you out of your default lens. It asks: what would someone else do in this situation, and why? Whether you're playing a war strategist or a startup founder in a simulated pitch meeting, you have to account for different motives, backgrounds, and logic systems.

Facilitated Add-On: Incorporate structured reflection:

- What surprised you about your role?

- Where did you lean into stereotype?

- How did your character's goals conflict with your own instincts?

You don't need a shelf full of board games to benefit. You need intention. The right game, paired with post-play reflection, becomes a micro-lab for testing your reasoning under real cognitive load. It's experiential learning in its sharpest form, fun, frustrating, and full of honest feedback.

So play. But play with purpose. Because when used right, games don't just entertain. They train your mind to notice, adapt, and think.

Reflective Prompts for Personal Growth in Decision-Making

Reflection isn't just looking back. It's building the habit of looking inward before you act.

Most bad decisions don't feel bad when you make them. They feel rushed, justified, or overdue. You're overwhelmed. You're trying to do the right thing fast. And you miss what your own mind is doing beneath the surface, projecting, defending, avoiding.

That's where reflective prompts come in. They create a pause in the noise. A mirror, not a moral. A way to see your habits before they hijack your choices.

Below are five categories of prompts designed to sharpen decision awareness. Use them as part of a weekly journaling habit, a self-check before major decisions, or even as questions to ask during team retrospectives. The goal isn't just better decisions, it's better thinking about decisions.

1. Pre-Decision Prompts: Catching the Mind Mid-Move

- *"What am I trying to avoid by making this choice quickly?"*

- *"If this turns out to be a mistake, what would I wish I had asked myself now?"*

- *"Whose voice am I trying to please, or silence, with this decision?"*

Purpose: These help you detect the emotional pressure driving the urge to act. You're not deciding yet, you're inspecting what's pulling you.

2. Clarity Prompts: Getting Specific About the Problem

- *"What exactly am I solving for?"*

- *"Is this a decision, a distraction, or a reaction?"*

- *"What outcome do I want, and what outcome am I prepared for?"*

Purpose: Often we're clear on the urgency but vague on the stakes. These prompts force precision. They separate urgency from clarity.

3. Bias Checks: Challenging Your Narrative

- *"What's one assumption I haven't tested?"*

- *"Am I overvaluing information because it came from someone I like, or dismissing it because it didn't?"*

- *"What would I advise someone else to do in this situation?"*

Purpose: Your thinking is always telling a story. Bias checks help you spot where the plotline is rigged. The third-person prompt is especially effective for shaking loose emotional entanglement.

4. After-Action Prompts: Reviewing the Ripple

- *"What did I learn about how I respond under stress?"*

- *"What surprised me, about the situation or myself?"*

- *"If I had to make this choice again, what would I do the same? What would I change?"*

Purpose: These reinforce a growth mindset without slipping into self-punishment. The idea isn't to judge your past, it's to extract insight for next time.

5. Long-Arc Prompts: Aligning with Identity and Purpose

- *"Does this choice reinforce the kind of person I want to become?"*

- *"Am I solving the short-term problem at the cost of the long-term goal?"*

- *"Where is fear showing up here, and how am I managing it?"*

Purpose: These widen the lens. They remind you that good decisions aren't always efficient. Sometimes the best move is the one that fits your values, even if it costs you comfort or speed.

You can't reflect on everything. But you don't need to. One well-timed question can shift your mental gear just enough to avoid a crash. And over time, that shift becomes a habit, a brief moment of clarity before the reflex kicks in.

You won't always make the right decision. But with these prompts, you'll know why you made it. And that's where growth lives, not in perfection, but in the pause between stimulus and choice.

Case Study Simulations for Real-World Application

Reading about critical thinking is easy. Living it, under pressure, with moving parts and incomplete information, isn't.

That's why simulations matter.

They build the bridge between theory and action through real-world messiness without the hypothetical fluff. You're given context, constraints, and conflicting inputs. You have to choose, knowing full well that your choice might backfire. But that's the point. Simulations create cognitive heat. And that heat reveals your blind spots, your instincts, and your ability to recalibrate in motion.

This section outlines how to use case study simulations to sharpen decision-making and problem-solving across five essential domains: leadership, ethics, collaboration, crisis, and innovation.

1. Leadership Simulation: The Overloaded Manager

Scenario:

You've just been promoted to manage a team of five, two high performers, one new hire, one chronic underperformer, and one who's technically skilled but toxic in meetings. Your supervisor wants results. Your team wants boundaries. You have 30 days to hit a major milestone or risk losing a critical client.

Your Task:

- Outline your top three priorities for the first two weeks.

- Decide how you'll handle the toxic but skilled employee.

- Present your plan to upper management, justifying trade-offs.

Debrief Prompts:

- Where did you spend most of your mental energy, results or relationships?

- What assumptions did you make about team members' motivations?

- Did you favor a familiar leadership style, and did it fit this context?

2. Ethics Simulation: The Whistleblower Dilemma

Scenario:

You discover that a senior colleague has manipulated data in a high-stakes report that influences stakeholder investment. You're not directly responsible, but you know. Reporting it could derail your career. Staying silent could harm the organization long-term.

Your Task:

- Identify your decision and the steps you'll take.

- Evaluate possible consequences from personal, organizational, and public perspectives.

- Justify your course of action using at least one ethical framework (e.g., utilitarianism, virtue ethics, duty-based ethics).

Debrief Prompts:

- Where did you feel torn, and why?

- Did you seek clarity or comfort in your ethical reasoning?

- What role did fear play in your choice?

3. Collaboration Simulation: The Stalled Project

Scenario:

You're on a cross-functional team that's missed two major deadlines. Communication is fragmented, and trust is low. Your team lead is overwhelmed and disengaged. There's growing pressure from stakeholders to "get it together."

Your Task:

- Design a strategy to reset the project without placing blame.

- Propose a new workflow model that addresses the root coordination issue.

- Anticipate resistance and outline how you'll address it.

Debrief Prompts:

- How did you diagnose the real problem?

- Did you default to control or collaboration?

- What assumptions did you make about others' willingness to change?

4. Crisis Simulation: The Sudden Turn

Scenario:

You're running a product launch that's been in development for six months. The night before release, a serious technical flaw is discovered. Fixing it will delay launch by three weeks and cost $40,000. Releasing now risks reputational damage.

Your Task:

- Make a go/no-go decision.

- Craft your communication strategy for both internal and external stakeholders.

- Identify how you'll mitigate fallout from either choice.

Debrief Prompts:

- What did you prioritize, reputation, cost, speed, or safety?

- Did you rationalize or reason your way through?

- How did stress affect your clarity?

5. Innovation Simulation: The Risky Pivot

Scenario:

You've pitched a bold new idea to your startup's board. They're intrigued, but only if you can validate the concept in 14 days. You've got limited budget, a small team, and no clear path to proof.

Your Task:

- Design a minimum viable experiment to test the idea.

- Choose what data you'll collect, what success looks like, and how you'll measure risk.

- Prepare your follow-up pitch for day 14, success or failure.

Debrief Prompts:

- Did you pursue simplicity or chase perfection?

- What risks felt worth taking, and why?

- Where did you trade certainty for speed?

Each simulation mirrors the friction of real life: time pressure, incomplete data, emotional stakes, and competing values. They're not meant to produce "correct" answers. They're meant to force visibility, on how you think, where you default, and what you need to refine.

You don't grow by memorizing frameworks. You grow by navigating fog. Case study simulations don't clear that fog, but they give you tools to walk through it with more clarity, more courage, and fewer collisions.

6

Emotional Intelligence and Team Dynamics

Emotional Awareness as a Catalyst for Team Cohesion

A team doesn't fall apart because of deadlines or differing opinions. It falls apart because no one notices, or admits, what's happening underneath. The tension in the room. The disengaged silence. The too-fast agreement that masks resentment. What derails collaboration isn't a lack of skill. It's a lack of awareness.

That's where emotional intelligence steps in. It functions as a core operational asset, not a peripheral soft skill. Emotional awareness, the ability to recognize, interpret, and respond to your own emotions and those of others, is foundational to any team that wants to do more than just coexist.

Without it, people default to reaction. With it, they move with intention.

The Invisible Glue of High-Performing Teams

We love talking about high-functioning teams in terms of productivity: *"They ship fast," "They iterate well," "They hit KPIs."* But those are symptoms. Not sources.

What makes these teams click isn't just processes, it's attunement. A shared emotional fluency that allows people to sense friction before it erupts. To know when someone's checked out or carrying more than they're saying. To recognize when a "no" is really a "not yet" and a "fine" is anything but.

That kind of cohesion doesn't come from off-sites or personality assessments. It comes from emotional presence. From people who pay attention, not just to tasks, but to tone. From leaders who ask, "How are we doing?" and mean it.

Start With You, Not Them

Too often, we treat emotional intelligence as something you use on other people, like a tool. But cohesion starts with self-awareness. If you don't know what's driving your own reactions, you can't show up clearly for anyone else.

Ask yourself:

- What happens to my communication when I'm under stress?

- How do I respond to conflict, shutdown, sarcasm, control?

- Am I aware of how my energy affects others?

The emotionally aware team member isn't the one who's always calm. It's the one who owns their emotional state and takes responsibility for how it shows up. They speak from experience, not defensiveness. They check in, not out. And they know when to pause because they're choosing not to escalate it.

Reading the Room, Not Just the Rules

Many team dysfunctions stem from a failure to read the emotional context. We assume people will "speak up if there's a problem." But that's a flawed premise. In many team cultures, honesty carries risk. Disagreement is discouraged. And silence is safer than conflict.

Emotionally aware teams make room for discomfort. They know the difference between harmony and suppression. This isn't about stirring up drama. They actively surface unspoken concerns, to prevent disconnection.

That might look like:

- Checking in with the quietest person in the meeting and asking for their take.

- Naming tension when it shows up instead of dancing around it.

- Modeling vulnerability as a strength, not a liability.

A team that reads the room well doesn't need everything to be perfect. They just need it to be real.

Awareness Leads to Adaptability

One of the most underappreciated benefits of emotional awareness is adaptability. Teams that track emotional tone can pivot, not just in workflow, but in relationship. If someone's burned out, emotionally attuned colleagues adjust. They don't punish. They don't pretend not to notice. They realign expectations with empathy.

This isn't about coddling. It's about strategic sensitivity. You want your team to be agile, flexible. That requires knowing when to push and when to hold. When to ask for more and when to create space. Emotional awareness makes that possible.

Because without awareness, we lead by assumption. And assumption is a poor substitute for intelligence.

From Awareness to Alignment

Team cohesion isn't about always getting along. It's about staying connected even when things get messy. Emotionally aware teams are rupture-resistant. They recover faster because they address what's real. They don't let small resentments fester into big problems. And they build trust by staying responsive, rather than reactive.

A cohesive team isn't a team without conflict. It's a team that metabolizes conflict before it turns toxic.

And it starts with this simple skill: noticing.

- Who's checked out?

- Who's overloaded?

- Who hasn't spoken in three meetings, and why?

- What aren't we saying right now?

Ask the questions. Hold the space. Build the habit of paying attention, not just to tasks, but to temperature. That's emotional awareness. And it's the thread that holds the team together when everything else feels like it's coming undone.

Managing Conflicts through Emotional Intelligence

Let's be blunt: conflict isn't the problem. Avoidance is. So is escalation. So is pretending your tone didn't carry judgment or that your Slack message didn't land like a slap.

Most team meltdowns don't happen over the issue itself, they happen because people were emotionally unprepared to handle disagreement. That's what makes emotional intelligence not just helpful but essential. It's the difference between constructive confrontation and corrosive silence. Between saying what needs to be said, and blowing up the room to do it.

Emotional intelligence doesn't mean you get everything right. It means you know what's happening inside you before it turns into behavior. It means you can spot your triggers, take a beat, and speak from clarity, not ego.

Conflict Is Data, Not Danger

Too many professionals treat conflict like a sign of failure. In reality, it's feedback. A live diagnostic on what's misaligned, expectations, communication styles, workloads, values. And like all good data, it needs interpretation. If you ignore it, distort it, or pretend it doesn't exist, the system keeps breaking down.

Emotionally intelligent teams don't run from conflict. They get curious about it. They ask questions like:

- What's actually being threatened here, status, autonomy, clarity?

- Am I reacting to what was said, or how it was said?

- What emotional baggage just got activated, and is it even relevant?

They understand that conflict isn't an interruption of work. It is the work. Especially in high-stakes, high-output environments where personalities clash and stress runs hot.

Spot the Emotional Undercurrent

The surface story, the missed deadline, the vague deliverable, the side comment in a meeting, is rarely the full picture. There's usually an undercurrent: someone feeling disrespected, dismissed, or misunderstood.

And here's where emotional intelligence changes the game. Instead of reacting to the content of the conflict, emotionally intelligent individuals respond to the emotional context:

- *"You cut me off twice in that meeting" becomes:*

  - *"I felt dismissed in the conversation and want to make sure my perspective is heard."*

- *"This team never listens" becomes:*

  - *"I'm frustrated because I don't feel like my input is being integrated."*

This shift isn't semantic. It's strategic. It moves the focus from accusation to insight. From blame to ownership. From *"you always"* to *"here's what's true for me."*

Emotionally intelligent language doesn't dilute feedback, it disarms defensiveness.

The Three Layers of Team Conflict

Not every team conflict looks the same. But they tend to fall into three broad layers, each with a different emotional demand:

1. Task Conflict

These are arguments about the work: what's being done, how, when, and by whom. Without emotional awareness, these devolve into turf wars. With it, they become opportunities for clarity.

Try:

- *"Can we walk through where our expectations diverged?"*

- *"Help me understand what your priorities were when you made that call."*

The goal isn't to agree. It's to understand the logic behind the choices.

2. Relational Conflict

This is where things get personal. Passive-aggressive remarks, exclusion from meetings, tone-policing, this kind of conflict stems from unmet interpersonal needs: respect, inclusion, recognition.

Try:

- *"I felt shut down earlier and want to clear the air."*

- *"I value our collaboration and don't want lingering tension to derail it."*

These conversations don't always feel natural. But the longer you delay them, the harder they are to repair.

3. Values Conflict

These are the most charged. It's not just about the what, but the why. One team member values transparency, another favors diplomacy. One wants speed, another prioritizes precision. Neither is wrong, but the mismatch can feel like betrayal.

Try:

- *"It sounds like we're coming at this from two different value sets. What's most important to you in this situation?"*

- *"Let's identify the shared goal, even if we're approaching it differently."*

With value conflict, emotional intelligence means recognizing that disagreement doesn't equal disrespect. It just means you care about different things, and both might be valid.

Emotional Intelligence in Action: Key Phrases That De-escalate

Sometimes conflict gets stuck not in substance, but in delivery. Here's how emotionally intelligent communicators turn down the heat without backing down:

Default Reaction | Emotionally Intelligent Reframe

- *"That's not what I said."* | *"Let me clarify what I meant."*

- *"You always do this."* | *"I've noticed this pattern, and it concerns me."*

- *"That's not fair."* | *"Can we look at how that decision was made?"*

- *"Why didn't you check with me first?"* | *"Next time, I'd appreciate being looped in sooner."*

- *"You're overreacting."* | *"This clearly matters to you, let's unpack it."*

These reframes aren't about being nice. They're about being effective. When tone matches intent, people stay in the conversation.

Turning Conflict Into Culture

Conflict isn't a problem to solve. It's a signal to decode. When handled well, it doesn't just prevent dysfunction, it builds trust.

Over time, your team learns that disagreement isn't dangerous. It's expected. It's manageable. And sometimes, it's the only way to break through to better ideas.

The highest-functioning teams don't eliminate conflict. They normalize it. They create norms around how to disagree, not whether it's allowed. That might mean:

- Weekly check-ins where feedback is built into the structure.

- A running "team friction log" where emerging tensions are documented neutrally.

- A commitment to speak to, not about, someone when issues arise.

Emotional intelligence doesn't mean everyone becomes best friends. It means they stay honest, clear, and connected, even when it's hard. Especially when it's hard.

Because the real skill isn't conflict resolution.

It's conflict fluency.

Building Empathy for Better Team Collaboration

You don't have to agree with someone to understand them. But if you can't understand them, you can't collaborate with them, at least not well.

Empathy isn't about being emotional. It's about being attuned. About recognizing that people aren't just bundles of output, they're shaped by experiences, pressures, insecurities, and goals you may never see unless you ask. In high-functioning teams, empathy is what turns friction into forward motion. It's the difference between "Why are you like this?" and "What might be going on for them?"

If emotional intelligence is the umbrella, empathy is the thread that weaves people together underneath it.

What Empathy Isn't

Let's clear something up right away: empathy is not pity. It's not forced agreement. It doesn't require you to carry someone else's emotional load or nod along with choices you fundamentally disagree with.

Empathy is perspective-taking. It's the discipline of imagining the internal world of another person and considering how your actions, tone, and choices might land for them. It's also a powerful form of pattern recognition: understanding how a teammate's behavior today might be linked to yesterday's stress or tomorrow's fear.

This kind of awareness doesn't slow a team down, it prevents derailment. Because once people feel understood, they stop defending their position and start contributing to solutions.

Tactical Empathy in Action

Empathy at work is not a feeling, it's a practice. Here are three simple ways to integrate it into daily team dynamics:

1. Ask Before You Assume

Default to curiosity. Instead of reacting to behavior, ask yourself:

"What pressure might they be under?"

"What would make me act that way?"

"Is this really about me, or is something else driving this?"

This internal pause disrupts your own bias and prevents unnecessary escalation. You move from conclusion to inquiry.

Then ask out loud:

- *"You seemed a little off in that meeting, want to talk about it?"*

- *"That response surprised me. Can I ask where it's coming from?"*

People won't always open up. That's fine. The point isn't disclosure. The point is creating space for connection, even if it's brief.

2. Mirror Without Mimicking

When people are stressed, they don't want you to match their panic. But they do want you to match their tone of urgency, or their need for calm. That's where empathy becomes situational fluency.

If a teammate is spiraling, your steady presence does more than advice ever could. If someone's stonewalling, your gentle persistence signals safety.

Empathy doesn't mean turning into a therapist. It means adjusting how you show up, your timing, tone, and expectations, based on what someone else might need in the moment. That's not coddling. That's influence.

3. Respond, Don't Redirect

One of the fastest ways to kill morale is by skipping emotional responses and jumping straight into solutions:

- *"Well, just tell them next time."*

- *"No big deal, right?"*

- *"You're probably overthinking it."*

These aren't helpful. They're invalidating.

Try this instead:

- *"That sounds frustrating."*

- *"I can see why that threw you off."*

- *"Want to walk through how that played out?"*

Validation isn't agreement. It's acknowledgment. It says, I see what this meant to you, even if I'd react differently myself. That's empathy in real-time, and it builds trust faster than any icebreaker ever could.

Empathy as an Efficiency Multiplier

There's a myth that empathy slows things down. That we should focus on tasks and leave emotions at the door. But that's not how people work. When team members feel unseen, they withdraw, or worse, retaliate in subtle ways: missed deadlines, minimal effort, behind-the-scenes resistance.

Empathy reduces that friction. It surfaces unspoken blockers. It prevents misunderstanding from calcifying into resentment. And it allows teammates to ask for help before they're overwhelmed.

Consider the alternative. Teams without empathy end up paying for it later, through miscommunication, turnover, burnout, and drama that could have been diffused early.

Empathy isn't inefficient. It's preventative maintenance.

Building a Culture of Empathy

If you want a culture where empathy sticks, you can't just model it in crisis. You have to embed it in the routine:

- Daily stand-ups: Make space for emotional check-ins, not just progress reports.

- Project retrospectives: Include *"how did we feel during this sprint?"* not just *"what went wrong?"*

- Conflict debriefs: Ask *"what mattered most to you in that moment?"* not just *"how do we fix this?"*

And above all, reward the behavior you want to see. Praise the person who calmed tension without backing down. Acknowledge the team member who asked a hard question with care. Highlight moments when empathy changed the outcome. Because in any team, what gets celebrated gets repeated.

The Bottom Line

Empathy isn't a bonus skill for managers. It's the baseline for everyone who wants to do collaborative work in a complex world. You don't need to be an emotional genius. You just need to care enough to pause.

You'll still miss cues. You'll still misread moments. But with practice, your default shifts, from judgment to curiosity, from assumption to understanding.

And that shift, repeated across a team, creates a culture where people don't just work together.

They show up for each other.

Strategies for Balancing Emotional and Logical Inputs

Let's be honest: most people default to one side. Some overanalyze and detach from what they feel. Others trust their gut, then reverse-engineer logic to justify the decision. Neither extreme works in the long run, especially in team settings where multiple perspectives collide under pressure.

Real-world problem solving isn't just about logic. And it's not just about emotion. It's about learning when to lead with data and when to listen to discomfort. It's about knowing that a technically correct answer that alienates people is still the wrong move.

Balancing emotional and logical inputs isn't about compromise. It's about integration. You don't mute one to hear the other. You train yourself to hear both, clearly, usefully, and in context.

The False Binary: Logic vs. Emotion

There's an old myth in professional culture that emotion clouds judgment and that real decision-makers keep their feelings in check. That's not clarity, that's distortion.

Emotions carry information. Anxiety might be alerting you to risk. Excitement might be pointing toward creative alignment. Resentment might be flagging a boundary violation. The key isn't to suppress these signals but to interpret them alongside your data.

Logic gives you structure. Emotion gives you motive. Ignore either, and you're solving the wrong problem.

Consider this:

Scenario / Logical Input / Emotional Input / Balanced Decision

Launching a new product under deadline / *"We're 10 days behind schedule."* / *"The team is visibly burned out."* / Delay by 5 days, scale back scope slightly.

Promoting a team member / *"She hits every metric."* / *"Others feel intimidated by her tone."* / Promote, but include a coaching plan.

Responding to critical feedback / *"They misunderstood the report."* / *"I feel defensive and misjudged."* / Clarify calmly, ask what confused them.

A purely logical decision may hit the target, but miss the context. A purely emotional decision may feel right, but collapse under scrutiny. Balanced input keeps you both effective and human.

The 4-Stage Calibration Method

To integrate logic and emotion without letting either dominate, use the following calibration method. It's simple, repeatable, and team-friendly.

Stage 1: Pause and Name the Emotion

Before reacting or solving, stop. Ask yourself (or your team):

- What emotions are showing up right now?

- Whose emotions are loudest, and whose are missing?

Name them without judging them. "Frustration," "relief," "worry," "pressure." Naming defuses. Suppressing amplifies.

Stage 2: Extract the Emotional Data

Ask:

- What is this emotion telling us?

- Is it based on past patterns, real-time feedback, or projected fear?

Treat emotion like input, not instruction. It belongs in the discussion, but not alone in the driver's seat.

Stage 3: Layer the Logical Framing

Now bring in the data:

- What are the actual constraints?

- What are the knowns, unknowns, and assumptions?

This is where you apply frameworks, SWOT, cost-benefit, first-principles thinking. Don't silence the emotions. Just give them structure to move through.

Stage 4: Make the Decision Explicitly Integrated

Choose a course of action that:

- Accounts for the emotional temperature

- Holds up under scrutiny

- Preserves relational capital and forward momentum

Then name why you're choosing it. For example:

"We're moving forward with the plan because the risks are quantifiable, and the team feels heard after adjusting the timeline."

This kind of explanation builds trust. People don't need to win every argument, they need to know their input mattered.

Team Habits That Encourage Balanced Thinking

It's hard to balance logic and emotion if your team only values one. Here's how to embed both in your team's culture:

- Normalize emotional language: Make it safe to say, *"This decision makes me uneasy, and I'm not sure why yet."*

- Use structured decision-making templates: Always include an "emotional impact" column in planning docs.

- Build reflection into post-mortems: Don't just ask *"What went wrong?"*, ask *"How did we feel during the process?"*

- Invite dissent and doubt: Logical critique and emotional discomfort both need a seat at the table. Don't confuse agreement with alignment.

When teams know that both their rational and intuitive sides will be respected, they stop gaming the system. They stop pretending to be fine when they're not. And they stop withholding good ideas because they don't "sound smart enough."

Balanced teams surface deeper truth, faster.

What to Watch For

Even in emotionally intelligent cultures, the balance can tip too far. Here are signs your team might be skewing:

- Skew Toward Logic / Skew Toward Emotion

- No room for dissent or uncertainty / Constant pivoting, lack of clear direction

- Overreliance on metrics / Decisions based on mood or intuition

- Dismissiveness of "soft" concerns / Dismissiveness of "hard" data

- Delayed action due to overanalysis / Premature action without full context

Both types of imbalance reduce trust. One makes people feel invisible. The other makes them feel unsafe. Neither is sustainable.

The Real Power of Balance

When you stop treating logic and emotion as rivals, you unlock decisions that are both sound and resonant. You stop swinging between cold analysis and hot reaction. You begin to lead, not just with intellect, but with wisdom.

In a high-speed, high-stakes environment, that's the edge. Not just being right.

Being right and relational.

Enhancing Team Morale with Emotional Insights

You can't schedule morale. You can't mandate it, budget it, or fake it. But you can feel it.

Morale isn't about team spirit or corporate slogans. It's the quiet pulse of a team's emotional life. It shows up in energy levels, risk tolerance, creativity, and how people respond when things go wrong. High morale doesn't mean everyone's happy all the time. It means people feel connected, motivated, and valued, especially under pressure.

And that starts with emotional insight.

Emotional intelligence isn't just for conflict mediation or tough conversations. It's a morale engine. Because when leaders and teammates understand the emotional undercurrents of their team, they don't just fix problems. They prevent them. They don't just reward output. They cultivate ownership.

Morale Is Made in the Micro-Moments

Forget the big offsite. Forget the quarterly town hall. The real drivers of morale happen in hallway conversations, team huddles, and five-minute check-ins.

When a team member shares an idea and isn't ignored, that's morale.

When someone's mistake is met with curiosity, not humiliation, that's morale.

When a new hire feels safe asking a "dumb" question, that's morale.

These small, emotional signals either reinforce trust, or erode it. And people are always keeping score, whether they admit it or not.

If you want to strengthen morale, don't chase vibes. Tune into the emotional math of your team:

- Who feels overlooked?

- Who's pulling more than their share?

- Who's not saying what they really think?

Morale issues often begin in silence. Emotional insight helps you hear the volume on what isn't being said, yet.

The Four Levers of Morale

Use these emotional insight levers to influence morale without relying on forced enthusiasm or toxic positivity:

1. Recognition that Lands, Not Just Looks Good

People don't need applause. They need to feel seen.

Generic praise (*"Great job, team!"*) fades fast. Targeted recognition sticks:

- *"You caught that bug before it went live, that saved us hours. Thank you."*

Emotional insight helps you match recognition to individual preference. Some want public acknowledgment. Others prefer a quiet message. Some need affirmation to feel secure. Others need trust to feel empowered.

Morale rises when appreciation feels accurate, not obligatory.

2. Rest That's Modeled, Not Just Permitted

Nothing kills morale faster than leaders who say *"take care of yourself"* but never log off.

Your team watches how you treat your own limits. If you glorify exhaustion, they'll suppress their own burnout. If you cancel a meeting to give people an hour back, they'll remember. Not because it's a perk, but because it signals that their capacity matters more than your optics.

High-morale teams don't just have PTO policies. They have emotional permission to use them.

3. Repair After Rupture

Mistakes will happen. Tension will build. Someone will snap. That doesn't tank morale, how it's handled does.

Teams with high morale don't fear missteps because they trust recovery. Emotional insight fuels that trust. It lets you say:

- *"I realized I dismissed your idea too quickly yesterday. That wasn't fair."*

These moments of repair build psychological safety. They signal that the emotional climate matters, and that rupture isn't the end of the relationship, just a moment to reset it.

4. Purpose That Feels Personal

Morale isn't just a matter of mood, it's about meaning.

When people know why their work matters, their emotional investment increases. But here's the catch: not everyone connects with the same purpose.

- Some need impact: *"Who does this help?"*

- Others need mastery: *"What am I learning?"*

- Others crave growth: *"Where is this taking me?"*

Use emotional insight to tailor the purpose conversation. Don't assume the mission statement is enough. Make it personal, or morale will default to paycheck-level motivation, and that never lasts long.

Watch for Hidden Drains

Even emotionally intelligent teams can overlook the slow leaks in morale. Pay attention to these early warning signs:

- Increased cynicism or sarcasm (masked disengagement)

- Reluctance to volunteer or take initiative

- Surface-level agreement with no follow-through

- Emotional flatness in meetings, no frustration, no excitement, just... nothing

These aren't "attitude problems." They're morale signals. Responding with pressure won't fix them. Responding with insight might.

Ask:

- *"What's feeling heavy lately?"*

- *"What's not working that no one's saying?"*

- *"If morale dipped this week, what would you trace it to?"*

Even just asking these questions changes the atmosphere. People feel it when the emotional climate is taken seriously.

The Bottom Line

Team morale isn't about fun. It's about function. It reflects whether people feel safe to think, speak, and stretch without fear of invisible penalties. It reflects whether the emotional cost of showing up outweighs the reward of contributing.

And you can't solve it with a survey.

You solve it by noticing. By listening. By staying tuned to the emotional circuitry of your team and making small, strategic adjustments that reinforce trust.

Because in the end, morale isn't how people feel about the company.

It's how they feel about coming back to the team tomorrow.

Creating a Supportive Environment for Open Communication

Most teams don't suffer from a lack of communication. They suffer from a lack of safety in communication. The words are there, but they're filtered, performative, or painfully edited to avoid conflict, judgment, or fallout. That's not openness. That's survival.

Open communication isn't about frequency. It's about freedom, freedom to disagree, question, admit confusion, share ideas, and give feedback without bracing for punishment. A team's real strength isn't measured by how often they talk. It's measured by what they're willing to say.

And that starts with the environment you create.

Safety First, Honesty Second

It's easy to say "we value transparency." But if people get shut down, ignored, or penalized for being honest, those words are noise. Emotional intelligence gives you the lens to spot where safety breaks down, not just through what's said, but what's not said.

Consider:

- Who never challenges decisions, even when they disagree?

- Who goes quiet after feedback sessions?

- Who waits until one-on-ones to share what they really think?

These silences speak volumes. If your team doesn't feel safe speaking up, they'll adapt. They'll start filtering everything through "Will this come back to bite me?"

And once that fear sets in, innovation stops. Risk-taking stops. Even connection starts to decay. Because nobody can collaborate fully when they're watching their back.

Elements of a Supportive Communication Climate

Creating true openness isn't about being endlessly positive or conflict-averse. It's about establishing clear norms that make emotional expression and dissent normal, not exceptional.

Here's what that environment looks like:

1. Clarity of Expectations

Ambiguity breeds anxiety. People can't communicate openly if they don't know the rules of engagement.

- What's the expected turnaround on responses?

- When is it appropriate to escalate?

- What kinds of feedback are welcomed, and in what form?

Set these expectations out loud. Better yet, co-create them as a team. Psychological safety grows when the boundaries are known, shared, and respected.

2. Permission to Be In Process

Not every idea needs to be polished. Not every opinion needs to be final. If your team only hears from people once they've rehearsed and refined, you're missing the best part, the messy, generative middle.

Create space for:

- *"This might not be fully formed, but here's what I'm thinking..."*

Reward exploratory communication, not just decisive soundbites. People open up when they don't have to perform certainty.

3. Repair Mechanisms That Actually Work

In any open environment, things will get tense. Someone will overshare. Someone else will misread the tone. That's not failure, it's part of the process.

What matters is what happens next.

Supportive teams normalize circling back:

- *"I've been thinking about our exchange yesterday, can we talk more about it?"*

If there's no trusted path for repair, people will shut down after one bad moment. Not because they're fragile, but because they're paying attention.

4. Neutral Zones for Hard Topics

Some conversations need space outside the usual workflow. Dedicated retrospectives, asynchronous feedback tools, or anonymous input channels can surface things that would otherwise get buried.

But the key is follow-through. If people share and nothing changes, trust erodes faster than if you hadn't asked at all.

Use these tools as springboards, not placeholders.

5. Modeling from the Top

If leaders don't admit mistakes, no one else will. If they never ask for input, people assume it's not welcome. If they interrupt or dismiss, others will follow suit.

Supportive communication doesn't start with policy. It starts with practice. When people see honesty handled with grace and challenge met with curiosity, they follow that lead.

And when they don't, they adapt to the dominant culture, no matter what your values deck says.

How to Spot a Truly Open Team

Here's what it looks like in the wild:

Shallow Communication Culture / Supportive Communication Environment

Quick nods, few questions / Clarifying questions, constructive pushback

Conflict avoidance / Respectful disagreement welcomed

Silence after tough decisions / Dialogue around rationale and impact

Private venting / Publicly voiced concerns and ideas

Performance over honesty / Processed emotion and thoughtful expression

The difference isn't tone. It's trust.

When Communication Gets Risky, Lean In

Even in open cultures, some conversations will feel high-stakes: calling out microaggressions, flagging burnout, admitting personal struggles, challenging leadership decisions. These are the real tests of your environment.

Don't flinch. Invite it.

- *"Thank you for bringing that up. Let's talk more about what that's looked like."*

- *"I hadn't considered that angle, tell me more."*

- *"That's hard to hear, but important."*

The more you normalize discomfort, the more fluent your team becomes in truth-telling.

Because the point of open communication isn't ease.

It's evolution.

Final Thought: Open Doesn't Mean Always

Supportive environments respect both expression and boundaries. No one should be required to share beyond what they're ready for. Safety also means privacy, pacing, and choice.

The goal isn't to turn your workplace into a confessional. The goal is to make sure no one feels they have to lie, perform, or disappear in order to stay employed.

That's what builds true engagement.

That's what drives lasting trust.

And that's how high-performing teams stay honest, together.

7

Overcoming Common Challenges in Problem Solving

Navigating Information Overload with Clarity

Let's start with the obvious: there's too much information, and most of it is garbage. Open your inbox, scroll your feed, glance at the Slack backlog from a two-hour meeting, and there it is. Data masquerading as insight. Alerts disguised as relevance. You're not just managing tasks anymore. You're filtering noise to find signals, often without realizing how much mental energy that takes.

This isn't just inconvenient. It's dangerous. When we're overwhelmed by information, we stop making decisions and start reacting to whichever input is loudest. Urgency hijacks clarity. Shortcuts replace strategies. And we end up solving the wrong problem, or worse, solving nothing at all.

So how do you stay sharp when the inputs won't stop coming?

The Myth of "More Input, Better Output"

We've been sold the idea that staying informed is the same as staying ahead. But cognitive science says otherwise. According to research on cognitive load theory, working memory has a hard ceiling. Once you exceed it, comprehension and retention plummet (Sweller, 2011). You don't just get slower, you get dumber. You default to the familiar, lean on bias, and grab whatever idea seems plausible rather than what's actually useful.

Professionals drowning in dashboards, memos, and constant notifications often confuse volume with value. But here's the catch: more data doesn't lead to better decisions unless you have a framework to sort it.

Step One: Define What Matters Before It Arrives

Clarity is preemptive, not reactive.

The sharpest thinkers don't process information faster, they filter better. They decide in advance what qualifies as useful. They ask:

- What problem am I solving?

- What kind of information helps me solve that?

- What's just noise, even if it's interesting?

This kind of intentional filtering is a form of cognitive triage. You're not trying to retain everything. You're tagging and discarding fast, like a surgeon deciding which patients go to the ER and which can wait.

You can't outsource that judgment to an algorithm. Tools can sort by keyword. Only you can sort by relevance.

Step Two: Use Layered Prioritization

Don't try to rank everything linearly. That's not how the brain works under pressure.

Instead, use layered prioritization, stack information into three broad buckets:

- Directly Actionable – facts or tasks you must respond to now.

- Contextual – background info that may shape a decision but doesn't demand one.

- Irrelevant or Deferred – anything that feels urgent but isn't, or can wait.

This takes less than a minute once practiced. Example: if you're reviewing a new product rollout report, the sales projections might be directly actionable. The competitor analysis is contextual. The marketing email drafts? Deferred, unless they contain a red flag.

This isn't about ignoring information. It's about staging it so your brain doesn't choke on all of it at once.

Step Three: Shrink the Frame to See More Clearly

Ironically, narrowing your field of vision can increase your awareness.

The default habit in overloaded environments is to zoom out. *"Let's look at the big picture."* But if your view is already cluttered, that wide lens only creates more blur.

Instead, shrink the problem. Turn it into a single question, or better yet, a constraint.

- *"How would I explain this in one sentence?"*

- *"If I could only act on one variable, which would it be?"*

- *"What's the single assumption I'm making here?"*

Constraints act like bumpers in a bowling lane. They don't guarantee a strike, but they keep you from veering into irrelevant territory. And they give the mind something to push against, something tight enough to generate focus.

Step Four: Create a Decision Dashboard (Not a Data Dump)

If your brain is the processor, you need a visual operating system.

This doesn't mean more dashboards with more metrics. It means building a compact visual reference for whatever challenge you're working on. Something you can glance at in under 30 seconds and know what matters.

Use simple formats like:

- A three-column list: What I know / What I assume / What I need to verify

- A color-coded matrix: Urgency vs. importance

- A timeline: Past decisions → outcomes → next steps

You're not building this for archival use. You're building it to calm your thinking. To replace mental flailing with a fixed structure that lets you reorient quickly, especially under pressure.

Step Five: Protect Your Processing Window

None of this works if your environment is constantly stealing your attention.

Every toggle between Slack and your notes, every notification buzz during analysis, every attempt to *"just check this real quick"*, it's a micro-tax on your clarity. Researchers call this "attention residue" (Leroy, 2009), and it compounds. You lose up to 40% of your cognitive efficiency just from switching tasks.

So carve out windows, 20, 45, or 90 minutes, where inputs are locked down. No inbox. No tabs. Just the signal you've already chosen to follow.

Clarity doesn't come from more hours. It comes from cleaner ones.

Information overload isn't just a productivity issue, it's a thinking issue. And the solution isn't to try harder. It's to think cleaner. Not everything deserves your attention. Not everything is data. Learn to treat your attention like a resource, not a reflex.

Once you stop reacting to everything, you can finally focus on solving something.

Overcoming Decision Paralysis with Structured Frameworks

Some people freeze when they don't have enough information. Others freeze when they have too much. Either way, the result is the same: delay, indecision, anxiety masquerading as analysis. You tinker with the options, ask for one more opinion, revisit the pros and cons list, and still nothing moves.

This is decision paralysis. And it doesn't always look like failure. Sometimes it looks like diligence. Caution. Thoroughness. But underneath, it's fear in a lab coat. You're not gathering input. You're stalling.

Why? Because high-stakes decisions aren't just about outcomes. They're about identity. What if I choose wrong and look incompetent? What if I disappoint someone? What if I lose control of the narrative?

If you want to overcome decision paralysis, you don't need more courage. You need less friction. And that's what structured decision frameworks are for.

What Structured Frameworks Actually Do

A good framework doesn't make the decision for you. It shortens the path to clarity by narrowing the chaos. It forces you to stop weighing options endlessly and start defining what matters.

Frameworks work because they:

- Externalize the decision (offload it from your overwhelmed brain)

- Surface hidden criteria (what you're really optimizing for)

- Convert emotional clutter into concrete steps

Think of it like scaffolding. It holds the problem in place while you climb it, instead of slipping every time the weight shifts.

The "PACT" Model for Fast, Focused Decisions

Let's build one. The PACT Model is a stripped-down framework for high-effort, medium-urgency decisions, ideal for professionals who don't have a week to "figure it out" but want more rigor than flipping a coin.

- Priority – What outcome matters most?

- Alternatives – What real options do I have?

- Consequences – What does each option cost me (emotionally, reputationally, financially)?

- Timeline – How long do I have before the decision makes itself?

Write it out. Don't trust yourself to "just know." If you pause here and do nothing else, at least document the consequences. That's where most hidden fear lives, not in the decision itself, but in what it seems to represent.

When Logic Isn't Enough: Add Weighted Values

If every option feels equally valid, or equally awful, you're likely missing a weight factor.

Try this: assign each consequence a numeric value based on its impact (1–10) and your tolerance (1–10). Multiply them. The higher the score, the more emotionally charged that outcome is for you.

Example:

- Option A: Might fail publicly (Impact: 9 / Tolerance: 3) = 27

- Option B: Delays a major launch (Impact: 7 / Tolerance: 6) = 42

- Option C: Mildly frustrating to team (Impact: 4 / Tolerance: 8) = 32

Suddenly, your brain isn't trying to weigh abstract feelings. It's seeing patterns. You're quantifying fear instead of letting it dictate your move.

Beware the Trap of the "Perfect Choice"

Perfectionism is the most socially acceptable form of avoidance. It lets you believe your paralysis is noble, that you're just being careful. That if you wait long enough, the perfect answer will emerge.

It won't.

There is no perfect choice, only tradeoffs. The faster you accept that, the faster you start solving for what you can live with, not what eliminates all risk.

Professionals get stuck here because they tie their value to flawless outcomes. But mastery isn't perfection. It's choosing with intention, even when the terrain is foggy.

Make the First Five Minutes Matter

When you sit down to make a decision, you usually waste the first five minutes wading through thoughts, distractions, or trying to psych yourself up. Use that time better.

Here's a five-minute starter protocol:

- Name the decision in a sentence.

- Write down what's at stake, not just for the project, but for you.

- List your current options without judgment.

- Eliminate one obvious "no."

- Set a timer for 15 minutes. Decide by then or document what's missing.

The timer matters. Time pressure forces emotional clarity. It won't always lead to a final decision, but it will surface what's blocking one, fear, missing data, emotional discomfort, or misaligned incentives.

Learn to Decide Without Closure

One of the hardest skills in modern work is making peace with partial data. You won't always get confirmation. You won't always be right. And clarity might only come after the fact.

That's not a flaw in your process. That's the cost of forward motion.

Your job isn't to know everything. Your job is to move, to make the next intelligent guess, adjust, and refine. And if you're wrong, that's not the end of your credibility. It's the beginning of your learning curve.

Structured thinking is how you make big decisions feel smaller. It replaces anxiety with action because you're focused. You're not looking for the path with no risk. You're looking for the one where your next step is clear.

And sometimes, that's all you need.

Breaking Free from Conventional Thinking Patterns

Most people don't think outside the box because they don't even see the box. They think inside inherited routines, default scripts, and unspoken rules disguised as logic. They call it realism. Or efficiency. But it's not. It's inertia.

You were taught how to think long before you ever questioned it. And by the time a problem comes along that demands a different approach, the old habits feel familiar and correct. That's how conventional thinking traps you. It offers the illusion of soundness when, in reality, you're stuck circling the same assumptions that created the problem in the first place.

Creative problem solving doesn't require magic. It requires nerve, the willingness to question the frame, the process, and even the goal itself.

The Hidden Power of Constraints

Here's the paradox: most people believe constraints kill creativity. In practice, they're the fuel for it.

Try solving a problem with infinite time, budget, and support. Your brain stalls. The options are too open, the stakes too vague. But give it one absurd constraint, "solve this with no money," "explain this to a 6-year-old," "only use tools you already have", and something shifts. The brain starts hunting sideways.

Creativity isn't about thinking freely. It's about thinking differently within limits. And some of the best ideas you'll ever have will come from trying to solve a problem where the usual tools don't apply.

This is why frameworks like SCAMPER (Substitute, Combine, Adapt, Modify, Put to another use, Eliminate, Reverse) are powerful, they push you to intentionally distort the frame. Not to be clever. To escape the drag of conventional logic.

Default Patterns That Masquerade as Rationality

Let's name a few common traps:

- Binary Thinking: "It's either this or that." Reality usually has a third (or fifth) option.

- Sunk Cost Bias: "We've already spent so much, we have to keep going." No. You don't.

- Expert Blindness: "That's not how it's done in our field." Exactly why you're stuck.

- False Consensus: "Everyone agrees this is the best way." Groupthink isn't consensus. It's social convenience.

Conventional thinking rarely announces itself. It wears a lab coat. It speaks in familiar metrics. It passes as prudent. But ask yourself: if I couldn't use the standard solution, what would I try next?

That's your real answer. That's the edge.

Run a Pattern Interruption Drill

You don't have to wait for a crisis to practice flexible thinking. In fact, the best innovators disrupt their own thought loops on purpose. Try this quick exercise once a week:

- Identify one problem you've been tackling the usual way.

- Name your current assumptions. Write them down. All of them.

- Force yourself to flip or violate at least two.

  - If your plan assumes "fast delivery," try solving it with "delayed rollout."

  - If you assume "cost-effective," try "luxury-first" and see what you notice.

- Follow the thread. Ask what would change. Don't stop at *"that's unrealistic."* Go deeper: what would make it realistic?

The goal isn't to act on every outlandish idea. The goal is to expand your field of motion, so when your go-to path is blocked, you're not frozen. You already know how to pivot.

Steal from Other Domains

Sometimes, the most original ideas come from somewhere totally unrelated.

A software engineer might solve a workflow issue using principles from restaurant kitchen design. A marketing team might refine messaging by studying how comedians pace a punchline. A nurse might streamline documentation using lessons from aviation safety checklists.

This is called lateral thinking, borrowing from other fields to unlock stuck patterns in your own. And it works because it bypasses the logic traps baked into your own industry. You're not trying to outsmart the problem. You're trying to out-context it.

Ask:

- *Who else faces a similar challenge, even in a wildly different setting?*

- *How would they approach this with their tools?*

- *What can I steal and adapt?*

This isn't a gimmick. It's how real breakthroughs happen.

Let Go of Being "Right"

At the root of most stuck thinking is fear, not of the problem, but of being wrong. You don't want to sound naïve, look foolish, or risk ridicule. So you self-edit before the idea is even born. You cling to safe ideas because they feel intellectually defensible.

But here's the truth: the best problem-solvers aren't always right. They're in motion. They try, tweak, test, and adapt. They don't defend their assumptions, they examine them. They don't ask *"Am I right?"* They ask, *"What else might work?"*

That humility isn't weakness. It's cognitive agility. And it separates people who sound smart from people who solve things.

Breaking free from conventional thinking isn't about being wild or reckless. It's about refusing to let past patterns dictate future moves. You don't need to be a genius. You need to be willing to look foolish long enough to get somewhere no one else has gone.

That's what real creativity is: disciplined rebellion.

Handling Workplace Politics with Strategic Thinking

Most people don't want to talk about workplace politics. They treat it like a dirty secret, something beneath real professionals or outside the scope of "pure" problem solving. But let's be clear: if you ignore politics, you're not rising above it. You're losing to it.

Because politics isn't just gossip or power games. It's the invisible layer of incentives, personalities, and hidden agendas that shapes every decision in your workplace. You don't have to like it. But if you want to solve problems that stick, you need to learn how to navigate it.

Not by playing dirtier. By thinking sharper.

First, Drop the Fantasy of a Purely Rational Workplace

We love to imagine that decisions at work are made based on merit, logic, and shared goals. Sometimes they are. Often they aren't.

People push agendas. They protect turf. They hold grudges. They promote ideas not because they're better, but because they're safer, flashier, or politically convenient.

If you don't factor that into your problem-solving approach, you'll keep getting blindsided. Good ideas will die in committee. Clear plans will get buried. And you'll wonder why "common sense" didn't win.

It's not that the solution was wrong. It's that it wasn't strategically positioned.

Strategic Thinking Starts with Power Mapping

Start by asking: Who really holds influence here?

Not just by title, but by:

- Who others defer to in meetings

- Who controls the flow of resources or approval

- Who's trusted by both leadership and the team

- Who frames the problem and sets the language

That's your influence map. And you need it before you pitch, propose, or push any solution forward.

Because solving the technical problem is only half the work. The other half is solving the social conditions that allow the solution to live.

Align Before You Assert

Most professionals are taught to get clarity first, then speak up boldly. But in politically complex environments, boldness without alignment is riskier than silence.

The fix? Don't pitch. Pre-align.

Before the meeting, ask yourself:

- *Who's likely to resist this idea, and why?*

- *What do they value that my idea threatens?*

- *Can I adjust language or approach to meet their goals without diluting the solution?*

That's not manipulation. That's translation.

Your job isn't to outmaneuver people, it's to help them see how your solution supports what they already care about. If you can do that honestly, you're not playing games. You're building bridges.

Play the Long Game Without Losing Your Spine

If you want to be strategic, you need patience. Not passive waiting, intentional sequencing. That means you might:

- Float a partial version of your idea to test reactions.

- Let someone else champion the idea publicly, even if it's yours.

- Wait until a key leader signals readiness before pushing a stalled initiative.

None of that makes you weak. It makes you durable.

But here's the catch: strategic patience doesn't mean compromising your core values. It means knowing which battles to stage and when. You can't solve anything if you're frozen out of the room. And staying in the room sometimes means playing smarter, not louder.

Use Narrative, Not Just Data

Hard truth: data doesn't win political battles. Narrative does.

You can have bulletproof analysis and still lose if it doesn't land emotionally. The smartest thinkers in the room often lose to the ones who can frame the problem in a way others feel invested in.

So when you present a solution:

- Tell a story that connects the dots: what's the human cost of not acting?

- Show how this aligns with the organization's identity or future.

- Frame your idea as a collective win, not a personal victory.

This isn't fluff. It's political oxygen. Without it, even brilliant solutions suffocate.

Don't Mistake Cynicism for Wisdom

It's easy to get jaded. Once you've seen ideas sabotaged, good people passed over, or power used selfishly, the temptation is to check out, to become "above it all."

But that's not wisdom. That's surrender dressed as insight.

Being politically aware doesn't mean becoming Machiavellian. It means becoming effective. You don't have to manipulate, backstab, or perform. You just need to read the room, understand the players, and design solutions that survive the real landscape, not the ideal one.

Solving problems in the workplace is about leverage. About knowing how to move through invisible resistance without losing your integrity.

Smart isn't enough. Strategic is better.

Addressing the Fear of Change in Problem Solving

Most people don't resist solutions because they're bad. They resist because they're different. The new system might be better. The process might be smoother. The outcome might be stronger. But if the change threatens someone's sense of competence, control, or comfort, it won't land.

That's not irrational. That's human.

And if you're trying to solve a problem without accounting for that fear, yours or theirs, you're not solving the real problem. You're just replacing one kind of discomfort with another.

Change Isn't Just Tactical. It's Identity-Based.

Here's what rarely gets said out loud in the workplace: "If this change works, does that mean I was wrong before?"

Or worse: *"Does it make me obsolete?"*

Every problem-solving initiative, no matter how technical or process-driven, carries a silent emotional tag. It says: we're leaving something behind. And for many people, that something includes pieces of their identity, how they see their value, their role, their authority.

That's why even logical upgrades meet resistance. It's not about the spreadsheet. It's about the story.

If you want to move people through change, you need to speak to both.

Surface the Fear, Don't Suppress It

Most leaders try to counter fear of change with pep talks or data dumps. "Look at all the benefits!" "This will make your job easier!" "The future is here!"

But reassurance isn't regulation. When someone is afraid, they don't need a PowerPoint. They need their concern acknowledged and made manageable.

Ask directly:

- *"What's your biggest worry about this shift?"*

- *"What would help you feel more supported during the transition?"*

- *"What's one thing you'd want to preserve, even as things evolve?"*

That conversation takes ten minutes. Avoiding it costs months.

Create Transitional Anchors

People can tolerate more change than they think, if there's something stable to hold onto.

These are transitional anchors: routines, values, or structures that don't change even as systems shift. They signal, *"Not everything is different."*

Examples:

- Keeping key team rituals intact even if roles change

- Preserving the language or branding of a legacy system within a new interface

- Framing the new method as an evolution, not a rejection

Anchors calm the nervous system. They let people move without losing themselves.

Use the "Permission to Reframe" Principle

Sometimes the best way to address fear is to reframe what change represents. Not a threat, but a test. Not a loss, but a chance to recalibrate.

But people need permission to reframe, from you, from leadership, or from someone they trust. That doesn't mean telling them how to feel. It means offering language that helps them process the shift without shame.

Try:

- *"We're not saying the old way was wrong. We're saying the conditions have changed."*

- *"This isn't about replacing people. It's about upgrading the system around them."*

- *"Let's not frame this as failure. Let's frame it as adaptation."*

People don't need spin. They need psychological space to revise the story without collapsing their sense of worth.

Give People Agency, Even If It's Symbolic

One of the strongest predictors of resistance is a perceived lack of control. If people feel a change is being done to them instead of with them, even small shifts can feel massive.

That's why you must build in agency, even symbolic agency. Let them choose the implementation date. Let them vote on naming the new tool. Let them decide how training is rolled out.

These aren't distractions. They're stabilizers. They return a sense of ownership to people who feel like passengers in a vehicle they didn't choose.

And when people feel ownership, they stop resisting. They start protecting the solution as if it were their own.

Fear of change doesn't mean people are fragile. It means they're invested. But to move them forward, you have to honor what they think they're losing, not just what you think they're gaining.

Real problem-solving includes emotional terrain. And the best leaders don't bulldoze through it, they map it, walk it, and build trust along the way.

Developing Resilience Against Setbacks and Failures

There's no elegant way to say it: you will fail. Not once. Repeatedly. Especially if you're solving real problems and not just polishing slide decks. And the people who succeed long-term aren't the ones who avoid failure. They're the ones who metabolize it.

Resilience is the ability to stay cognitively engaged, emotionally regulated, and behaviorally functional, even after something doesn't go as planned.

And for most professionals, that's the part no one teaches you. You get trained to solve problems, but not to survive the backlash when the solution falls apart.

Let's fix that.

Setbacks Are Not Evidence You're Incompetent

High performers often misread failure as a referendum on their intelligence or capability. *"If I were smarter, I would've seen that coming." "If I were better, this wouldn't have blown up."*

That's shame talking, not strategy.

Most failures in complex environments aren't personal. They're systemic. A variable shifted. A stakeholder flipped. A resource vanished. And yes, sometimes you misjudged it. But that doesn't mean you're broken. It means you're working in the real world.

Reframing failure is step one. You're not here to be right all the time. You're here to learn fast and adapt better.

Create a Post-Failure Audit Ritual

Emotionally intelligent professionals don't wallow after a setback, but they also don't blow past it. They pause, assess, and mine it for learning.

Build this into your workflow:

- Name the event. (*"We launched a new feature that users ignored."*)

- List what went wrong. Stick to facts, not self-blame.

- Extract what you missed. What signs were there that you didn't act on?

- Re-state your process. What would you do differently, step-by-step?

- Decide how to test again. Not whether. How.

This turns failure from identity damage into pattern data. It moves the pain into motion.

Watch for the Resilience Killers

Some common mindsets quietly drain your resilience without you realizing it:

- **Catastrophizing:** turning one setback into a permanent label (*"This always happens to me."*)

- **Comparison spirals:** benchmarking your worst moment against someone else's highlight reel

- **Overcorrection:** swinging wildly in the opposite direction next time to avoid any resemblance of past failure

Each of these is a fear reflex dressed up as logic. They don't make you smarter. They make you rigid. And rigidity is the enemy of resilience.

The fix? Start with awareness. Notice when your internal story becomes absolute ("never," "always," "everyone else"). Then rewrite it like a data analyst, not a doomed poet.

Build a Personal Resilience Protocol

You can't control the storm, but you can control what you anchor to when it hits. Develop a protocol that helps you stabilize quickly after a setback.

Include:

- A cognitive reset (e.g., journaling facts vs. feelings)

- A support loop (one or two people who can reflect the truth, not just encouragement)

- A small win task (something you can complete in 15–30 minutes to rebuild agency)

- A reflection checkpoint (usually after 48–72 hours, to look back with distance)

This isn't about bouncing back instantly. It's about resuming motion before doubt sets in permanently.

Normalize Setbacks in Your Culture

If you're in a leadership role, your response to failure sets the tone. Do you treat it as an anomaly? A weakness? Or as part of the process?

Normalize reflection without punishment. Praise clean failure, the kind that came from trying, testing, and learning, not from negligence or laziness.

And model resilience yourself. Share your own stumbles without drama or ego. It sends a signal that failure isn't exile. It's exposure. And it's survivable.

Setbacks aren't the opposite of progress. They are progress, if you know how to use them. The real win isn't avoiding failure. It's staying intact when it finds you. Sharpened. Humbled. Still moving.

That's resilience. Not armor. Not denial. Just motion with your eyes still open.

8

Sustaining Growth and Continuous Improvement

Building a Growth-Oriented Mindset

M ost people don't fail because they're incapable. They fail because they stop. They stop learning. Stop adjusting. Stop engaging with complexity the moment it starts to bruise their ego. The first step to becoming someone who solves problems well, and keeps solving them, is realizing that mindset isn't a mood. It's a mechanism.

A growth-oriented mindset is not about cheerleading yourself into confidence. It's about operating from the belief that skills are expandable. And more importantly, that failure is diagnostic. This mindset isn't motivational fluff. It's a cognitive position, a way of interpreting feedback, mistakes, and plateaus that increases your capacity over time. If your instinct is to avoid hard truths, you'll keep solving the same problems in prettier wrappers. But if you learn to interpret friction as a signal, you'll access more solutions than most people even realize exist.

Let's break it down.

Growth Mindset Isn't Just About Belief, It's About Use

Psychologist Carol Dweck's research (2006) popularized the distinction between fixed and growth mindsets, showing how beliefs about intelligence shape motivation, resilience, and achievement. But in practice, belief alone doesn't move the needle. Plenty of people say they *"believe in growth,"* yet avoid every challenge that doesn't guarantee an ego boost. They sidestep feedback. They downplay others' success. They operate like image preservation is more important than actual improvement.

That's not growth. That's ego management disguised as development.

The real hallmark of a growth-oriented thinker isn't blind optimism, it's functional discomfort. It's the willingness to stay engaged even when the process gets messy, the outcomes are uncertain, and the learning curve scrapes your pride. Especially then.

Spotting a Growth-Oriented Problem Solver

Growth-minded problem solvers do a few things differently. They ask sharper questions. They invite contradiction because it prevents stagnation. They know most blind spots are invisible by definition, so they seek perspective like it's oxygen.

Here's what to watch for:

- **They revise quickly.** They don't wait for perfection to act, but they also don't cling to their first plan just to protect their self-image.

- **They normalize rework.** Instead of labeling revisions as failure, they see it as iteration. Just like a designer doesn't expect their first draft to ship, neither do they.

- **They track process, not just results.** Outcomes are important, but they study how they got there. What they did that worked. What they missed. What surprised them.

- **They detach from outcome identity.** Whether the solution worked or not doesn't alter their belief in their ability to improve. Ego doesn't glue them to a particular path.

Contrast that with fixed thinkers who often operate with binary logic: if they fail, they're "not cut out for this." If they succeed, they're "naturals." They either "have it" or they don't. And once that identity is on the line, the risk of trying something new becomes intolerable.

What Fuels a Growth Mindset, And What Sabotages It

Growth doesn't come from reading more books or stacking credentials. It comes from interpreting discomfort the right way. When something feels hard, it's not a sign that you're broken, it's a sign that the brain is doing what it's supposed to do: adapt. Neuroplasticity, the brain's ability to rewire itself through experience, is driven by effortful learning. The "click" comes after the mental friction, not before it.

But we sabotage this process in two major ways:

- **Over-identifying with being competent.** If your self-worth is tied to always being the smartest person in the room, you'll never risk looking dumb long enough to get smarter.

- **Interpreting feedback as attack.** Growth requires data. If you take every piece of feedback as a personal insult, you'll cut yourself off from the most useful learning source you have: other people's insight into your blind spots.

Instead, try using a question like, *"What is this experience trying to teach me?"* when you hit a wall. That one shift reframes failure as instruction, not indictment.

Practical Ways to Build and Maintain a Growth Mindset

You don't just "decide" to be growth-minded and wake up transformed. It's a skill set, like anything else, and it needs reinforcement. Here are a few methods that translate belief into behavior:

- **Run short feedback loops.** After every significant project or decision, debrief yourself. What worked? What didn't? What would you do differently? Write it down.

- **Practice learning aloud.** When someone asks how you got good at something, don't say, *"Oh, I've always been this way."* Break down the struggle. Model growth for others and it'll reinforce your own process.

- **Use challenge as calibration.** If nothing's hard, you're not stretching. If everything's hard, you're probably under-resourced. Find the tension point where difficulty equals growth, then live there.

- **Reframe setbacks as skill gaps.** *"I'm not good at this"* becomes *"I haven't developed that skill yet."* Language matters more than you think.

You can also surround yourself with people who challenge your thinking, not just echo it. Curate your input. Audit your environment. Growth requires exposure to ideas that feel unfamiliar, sometimes even uncomfortable.

Final Thought: Growth Isn't Endless Hustle, It's Directional

Growth-minded doesn't mean "never satisfied." It doesn't mean you have to turn every moment into a life lesson or burn out trying to optimize everything. Real growth has direction. It's about choosing what matters, getting better at it deliberately, and accepting the discomfort that comes with that journey.

Otherwise, you're just chasing dopamine and calling it progress.

The best thinkers don't just consume knowledge. They metabolize it. And that requires mindset, not motivation.

Continuous Learning and Adaptability in Problem Solving

Most people treat learning like a phase, something you do in school, in a training module, or when onboarding for a new job. Then they "graduate" from the uncomfortable part of growth and double down on what they already know. The problem is, the world doesn't freeze for your convenience. Systems evolve. Markets change. What worked last year starts to wobble. Suddenly, the person who knew everything about how things used to be becomes the one holding the team back.

Adaptability isn't a nice-to-have. It's a survival skill.

And continuous learning isn't about stuffing your brain with random knowledge. It's about recalibrating faster than the problems outpace you.

Learning as a Dynamic Toolset

Think of learning like software, not hardware. You're not collecting facts to install into your mental hard drive for permanent storage. You're updating a system that needs constant debugging and retooling. Every new situation is a variable test case. What works here might break there. The trick isn't to memorize more. It's to learn how to adjust your logic flexibly under changing conditions.

In the field of learning science, this is often referred to as transfer of learning, the ability to apply knowledge or strategies learned in one context to another. Rote learners struggle here. Adaptive learners don't. Why? Because they don't just absorb content. They absorb context.

A technical lead who learns how to debug a new software platform is doing more than memorizing syntax. They're learning how to approach unfamiliar systems, how to isolate a problem, test a theory, and iterate. That process matters more than the particulars of the program. Because tools change. Methods evolve. The mindset and method stick.

Adaptability Isn't Instant Flexibility, It's Structured Reframing

Some people think adaptability means "go with the flow." It doesn't. That's passivity. Real adaptability is deliberate. It means you assess what's changed, question whether your existing framework still fits, and then consciously decide how to respond.

Let's say your company adopts a new CRM tool. A fixed thinker grumbles: *"We've always done it this way."* An overwhelmed thinker panics: *"This is going to ruin everything."* An adaptable thinker asks: *"What's the learning curve, and how do I build a process that gets us through it with minimal friction?"*

This process has three repeatable parts:

- Awareness: Spot that change is happening, or needs to.

- Assessment: Compare new inputs to old frameworks. Where's the mismatch?

- Adjustment: Test a new approach and recalibrate as needed.

It's not about pivoting constantly. It's about pivoting intelligently, based on evidence, not panic.

How to Build a Habit of Continuous Learning

Lifelong learning sounds romantic. But in reality, it's messy, inconsistent, and often invisible. You'll have days where everything clicks. Others where it feels like you're walking backward through fog. That's not a bug. That's the process.

If you want to make learning a sustainable habit, treat it like compound interest. Small, repeated investments pay off over time. Here's how:

- **Schedule friction.** Make learning part of your routine, whether it's 15 minutes of reading, a weekly knowledge share with a colleague, or watching a case study breakdown every Friday. Don't rely on motivation. Rely on structure.

- **Track questions, not just answers.** Keep a running list of things you don't know. Then make time to find out. Curiosity compounds.

- **Reflect weekly**. What did you learn this week? What surprised you? What skill or insight did you apply that you didn't have six months ago?

- **Teach to learn.** One of the fastest ways to solidify knowledge is to explain it to someone else. You'll find the gaps faster than any test.

- **Bonus: Don't confuse information hoarding with learning.** Watching videos and reading articles all day without applying anything is intellectual procrastination. If you don't use it, you lose it. Application is the real learning loop.

Adaptive Problem Solvers Make Better Collaborators

There's another reason adaptability matters, it makes you easier to work with. Teams don't need heroes. They need adjusters. People who can step in, stay flexible, shift gears, and make things work without drama.

The adaptive problem solver doesn't blow up when the client changes direction. They regroup. They don't cling to sunk costs or spiral into nostalgia. They say, *"Okay, this is the new problem, what needs to happen now?"*

This orientation isn't just a personality trait. It's a learned skill. And it makes you a stabilizer during moments of chaos.

The Trap of Overconfidence, and the Antidote of Learning

There's a dangerous point in every professional's arc: the moment they get good enough to stop learning. They plateau. Routines take over. They start recycling old solutions out of habit, not relevance. And eventually, they fall behind.

This isn't because they got worse. It's because they stopped updating the problem set. Their toolkit froze in place.

The antidote? Stay uncomfortable. Not in a burnout way, but in a growth way. Surround yourself with people who challenge you. Chase contexts that stretch you. And when things get hard, don't assume you're failing. Assume you're learning something new, and the discomfort is a clue that it matters.

Final Thought: Evolve or Get Left Behind

Every skill degrades if it isn't sharpened. Every mindset calcifies if it isn't challenged. If you're not actively learning, you're silently declining. It's not a crisis. It's just entropy.

But the good news? Learning is renewable. Every day gives you a new chance to upgrade your operating system. You don't need to know everything. You just need to be the person who adapts faster than the world erodes your edge.

Adaptability is your long game. Learning is how you play it.

Leveraging Community and Collaboration for Growth

Problem solving doesn't happen in a vacuum. Even if you're the sharpest mind in the room, your perspective is limited by design. You can't see your own blind spots. You can't test every variable alone. And more importantly, you're not supposed to. Growth accelerates when you stop trying to be the smartest person in the room, and start learning how to think with the room.

Collaboration isn't just a feel-good value. It's a force multiplier. Used well, it turns individual competence into collective intelligence. But only if you learn how to wield it.

Community Isn't Groupthink, It's Cognitive Expansion

Too many people confuse collaboration with conformity. They think being a "team player" means never pushing back, always deferring, or sacrificing their judgment for the illusion of harmony. That's not collaboration. That's capitulation.

Real collaboration requires friction. The kind that sharpens. The kind that exposes gaps, refines logic, and challenges assumptions. When done right, it pushes ideas further than any one person could alone. Why? Because every brain brings a different filter. A different lexicon. A different set of priors.

You want diverse thinkers around you. People who approach problems from weird angles. People who make you rethink your defaults. People who don't just nod, they nudge.

A high-functioning team doesn't agree on everything. They agree on how to disagree without burning the place down.

Why Lone-Wolf Problem Solvers Get Stuck

Independence is admirable, until it becomes a liability. If your default mode is *"I'll figure it out on my own,"* you'll hit a ceiling. Fast. Here's why:

You miss critical input. Someone else has already solved a similar problem, or made the mistake you're about to make. Collaboration accelerates the feedback loop.

You burn bandwidth. Reinventing the wheel every time isn't noble, it's wasteful. Collaboration reduces cognitive load by spreading insight across shared effort.

You distort outcomes. Solving in isolation means your own biases go unchecked. You might optimize the wrong variable or ignore context you didn't even know was there.

There's a time for focused solo work. But if you're building anything that requires scale, influence, or innovation, you need others. Not as accessories. As accelerants.

Building a Collaboration Habit (Even If You Hate Meetings)

You don't need to be a social butterfly or host brainstorming parties. Effective collaboration is less about being extroverted and more about being structured. Here's how to integrate community into your problem-solving flow:

- **Create feedback checkpoints.** Don't wait until something's "done" to ask for input. Bake in scheduled touchpoints where you present rough drafts, test theories, or challenge assumptions.

- **Designate devil's advocates.** Appoint someone whose role is to test ideas in order to strengthen them. Normalize challenge as part of the creative process.

- **Use async tools.** Not every collaboration needs a live meeting. Use shared docs, voice notes, or Loom recordings to capture ideas without stealing people's calendars.

- **Clarify decision rights.** Know who's input is advisory vs. who holds the final call. Otherwise, collaboration turns into endless consensus loops with no traction.

The goal is to make feedback safe, dissent useful, and process clear.

Learning Through Collective Intelligence

Communities aren't just support groups, they're learning machines. A community of thinkers who push each other, share case studies, deconstruct failures, and experiment publicly is a faster track to mastery than years of isolated reading.

Want to level up your decision-making? Join a group where good decisions are deconstructed. Where someone asks, *"How did you land on that?"* and expects a structured answer. Want to think more creatively? Find a cohort that runs idea sprints. Want to navigate uncertainty better? Surround yourself with people who've failed publicly, recovered, and still ship bold work.

The quality of your questions improves when the people around you demand better questions.

Collaboration Without Dilution

There's a risk in every group setting: the temptation to dilute your own thinking to avoid conflict or to make the group dynamic easier. Don't. Effective collaboration doesn't require you to soften your edge. It requires you to temper it, sharpen it through interaction, not mask it for harmony.

Here's the distinction:

- Dilution says: *"I won't speak up because it might cause friction."*

- Temperance says: *"I'll speak clearly and respectfully, even if it causes friction, because clarity matters more than comfort."*

One leads to silence. The other leads to strength.

The best collaborative thinkers know when to yield, when to push, and when to pause. They're not always the loudest, but they are the most catalytic.

Final Thought: You Don't Need a Tribe, You Need a Circle

In a world obsessed with echo chambers and identity groups, it's easy to confuse belonging with agreement. Don't build a tribe that only mirrors you. Build a circle that tests you.

You need thought partners, the ones who challenge your ideas, sharpen your thinking, and ask better questions instead of nodding along. The right collaborative space doesn't just make you feel seen, it makes you smarter.

Growth is a team sport. And the best problem solvers don't go it alone; they build systems of minds that think better together than any one person could apart.

Tracking Progress and Measuring Success in Problem Solving

You can't improve what you don't measure. And yet, most people approach problem solving like a one-time event instead of a skill with trackable metrics. They solve something once, breathe a sigh of relief, and move on, never stopping to ask how they solved it, why it worked (or didn't), and whether their decision-making is actually evolving over time.

That's not growth. That's survival.

To sustain improvement, you need a system for tracking progress and defining success, one that goes beyond *"Did it work?"* and digs into how it worked, what changed, and what's repeatable.

Why Measuring Matters More Than Most Thinkers Realize

Measurement isn't about micromanaging your thought process. It's about capturing patterns, good and bad. It's how you diagnose recurring bottlenecks. How you learn which tools serve you and which ones sabotage you. And, most importantly, how you escape the trap of feeling "busy" without getting better.

When you measure your thinking, you:

- Spot when ego hijacks logic.

- Catch when analysis turns into avoidance.

- Recognize when *"sticking with it"* is grit, or just stubbornness in a new outfit.

Without measurement, you fall back on vibes. And vibes aren't a system.

What Should You Track? Not Just Outcomes, Decisions

The most obvious thing to measure is whether the problem got solved. But that's the lagging indicator. By the time you get the result, it's too late to fix the thinking that got you there.

Better to focus on leading indicators, clues from your process that reveal how you think, not just what you chose.

Here's what to track:

- Decision clarity: Did you define the actual problem, or just react to symptoms?

- Option generation: How many viable paths did you explore before acting?

- Bias checks: Did you challenge your first instinct or look for disconfirming evidence?

- Communication strategy: How effectively did you articulate the decision to others?

- Reflection loop: Did you debrief after the fact, or move on and hope for the best?

This isn't just for major projects. Apply it to weekly decisions, interpersonal challenges, even daily priorities. Over time, you'll start to see which part of your process creates the most drag, and which accelerates resolution.

Frameworks for Measurement: Make Progress Visible

You don't need a fancy dashboard or data scientist. A simple framework can make progress visible. Try one of these:

1. The Decision Journal

A decision journal is exactly what it sounds like: a record of key decisions you've made, why you made them, what you expected to happen, and what actually did. Over time, it reveals patterns in your thinking, how you respond under pressure, where your blind spots live, and how accurate your predictions really are.

Template:

- What is the decision?

- What are the options?

- What am I predicting will happen, and why?

- What's the worst-case scenario?

- What biases might be influencing me?

- What actually happened?

Update it periodically to check your calibration. It's a humbling, but wildly effective, exercise.

2. The Solve Cycle Tracker

For ongoing challenges or strategic goals, create a cycle tracker: a tool that documents your problem-solving cycle from definition to reflection. Think of it as a closed feedback loop.

- Cycle components:

- Problem Definition

- Hypothesis / Assumption

- Plan / Action Taken

- Result Observed

- Insight Gained

- Next Step

The key here isn't to hit a perfect score. It's to notice drift. Where do you regularly skip steps? Where does your attention collapse?

3. The Problem Heatmap

If you're solving problems across a team or company, consider mapping problems by frequency, severity, and recurrence. This helps you focus your energy on high-leverage issues rather than playing whack-a-mole with noise.

Categories:

- High frequency, low impact = automation targets

- Low frequency, high impact = contingency planning

- High frequency, high impact = top priority for innovation

This is especially useful for leaders who need to decide where to intervene and what to delegate.

Measuring Success Without Perfectionism

Don't confuse measurement with perfectionism. This isn't about chasing flawless results. It's about spotting progress, not pretending to be infallible.

A successful thinker isn't the one who makes the fewest mistakes. It's the one who learns from them the fastest. So your success metrics should include:

- **Time to pivot:** How quickly do you notice when something's not working and adjust?

- **Resilience rate:** How well do you recover after setbacks, emotionally and tactically?

- **Communication velocity:** How efficiently can you bring others into your thinking or mobilize action around it?

- **Pattern awareness:** Are you noticing recurring friction points in your thought process?

Track these. Not obsessively. Just often enough that you're not fooling yourself.

Final Thought: Build a Thinking OS, Not Just a To-Do List

Productivity culture teaches you to focus on tasks. But if you want to grow, focus on thinking systems. The people who get better over time aren't just efficient, they're calibrated. They know how they make decisions, where their reasoning holds up, and when to override their own instincts.

Don't just celebrate outcomes. Study them.

Because problem solving isn't about what you did. It's about how you think when it counts.

Future Trends in Critical Thinking and Decision Making

Critical thinking isn't a fixed skill, it's a moving target. As the world gets faster, louder, and more algorithmically curated, what counts as clear thinking keeps shifting. Yesterday's sharp decision-maker might drown in tomorrow's noise. And tools that worked five years ago might already be obsolete.

That's not a problem to fear, it's a reality to prepare for.

If you want to future-proof your problem-solving, you need to understand where the terrain is heading. Because staying sharp isn't about mastering today. It's about being ready for what comes next.

Trend #1: AI-Augmented Thinking

Artificial intelligence isn't replacing human reasoning, it's reshaping it. From generative language models to predictive analytics, AI is increasingly part of how we process information, spot patterns, and make decisions.

But here's the catch: AI excels at surfacing possibilities, not choosing among them. That's still a human job. And it requires sharper discernment than ever.

The future problem solver needs to:

- **Audit inputs.** Not all AI outputs are trustworthy. You'll need to ask, *"What data trained this model?"* and *"What bias might it reflect?"*

- Challenge automation. Just because something can be predicted doesn't mean it should be automated. Judgment is still your edge.

- Use AI as a collaborator, not a crutch. Let it expand your thinking, but don't outsource your ethics or intuition.

AI will help you generate options. It won't help you grow a backbone. That's on you.

Trend #2: Decision-Making in Ambiguity

We've left the era of linear planning. What used to be predictable now shifts mid-project. Industries transform overnight. One viral post can flip public opinion. One breakthrough can decimate a career path.

That means you need to think probabilistically, not categorically. The question isn't *"What's the right answer?"* It's *"What's likely to work, given what I know, and how will I update if I'm wrong?"*

That means:

- Getting comfortable with partial information.

- Running scenario models instead of binary forecasts.

- Staying agile without collapsing into indecision.

The best thinkers in this next era won't be the most confident. They'll be the most calibrated.

Trend #3: The Return of Embodied Intelligence

In a world obsessed with screen time and data dashboards, we're rediscovering something ancient: your body knows things your brain ignores. Stress responses. Energy shifts. Nonverbal cues. Gut-level misalignment.

This is more than "trust your gut." It's about integrating somatic cues into your cognitive process.

The future of critical thinking includes:

- **Somatic awareness:** Noticing when your body tenses, shuts down, or reacts before your mind does.

- **Emotional literacy:** Being able to differentiate between fear that's protective vs. fear that's paralyzing.

- **Regulation rituals:** Using breath, movement, or grounding practices to recover clarity before decision-making.

Cognitive clarity and nervous system regulation will no longer be seen as separate disciplines. They'll be core to any high-stakes thinking environment.

Trend #4: Values-Based Decision Frameworks

As trust in institutions declines and social complexity grows, more professionals are realizing: logic alone doesn't get you out of ethical gray zones. You need values.

We're moving into a decision landscape where frameworks must include not just *"What works?"* but *"What aligns?"*

You'll need to define:

- Personal red lines. What won't you compromise, even under pressure?

- Organizational ethics. What principles govern your

process, not just your goals?

- Impact awareness. Who benefits? Who's harmed? Who gets left out?

Clear values clarify decisions when data doesn't.

And no, values aren't fuzzy abstractions. They're operational filters. Treat them as such.

Trend #5: Cognitive Diversity as a Strategic Asset

If everyone on your team thinks like you, you're not building a high-performance unit, you're building a confirmation loop.

The next wave of problem solving will depend on cognitive diversity: thinkers who approach problems from different angles, with different priors, and challenge each other constructively.

That means:

- Hiring for difference, not comfort.

- Creating psychological safety for dissent.

- Training for meta-cognition, so team members can notice how they think, not just what they think.

This won't always feel good. But it will prevent blind spots that kill ideas, or companies.

Final Thought: Don't Just Prepare for the Future, Shape It

Most people try to future-proof their thinking by clinging to the past. That won't work. The world is iterating too fast. What you need is adaptability, values clarity, and a mental engine that can update without breaking.

The best decision makers in the next decade won't be those who memorize frameworks. They'll be those who can build new ones on the fly, while still staying grounded in their principles.

So stay curious. Stay humble. Stay uncomfortable.

Because the future doesn't reward people who know the most.

It rewards those who can think the clearest when it matters most.

The Role of Reflection in Sustaining Personal Growth

Some lessons don't show up until you slow down. You can read all the right books, chase every strategy, optimize every hour, but if you never stop to ask, *"What did this teach me?"*, growth stalls. Not because you stopped trying, but because you stopped absorbing.

Reflection isn't indulgence. It's integration.

It's the moment learning crystallizes into insight. It's how failure becomes useful, how patterns get spotted, and how problem-solving matures into wisdom.

Without reflection, you're not improving. You're just repeating.

Reflection vs. Rumination: Know the Difference

Let's clear something up: reflection is not rumination. One leads to clarity. The other leads to paralysis.

Reflection asks: What happened? Why? What can I learn? What changes next time?

Rumination loops: Why did I mess that up? What's wrong with me? Will I ever get it right?

Reflection is structured. Rumination is chaotic. Reflection leads to action. Rumination leads to self-doubt.

If your "thinking time" ends in shame instead of insight, it's not reflection, it's self-punishment disguised as analysis. Drop the whip. Pick up the pen.

How Reflection Sustains Long-Term Growth

Problem-solving isn't just about solving this problem, it's about solving the next one better. That requires memory. Pattern recognition. Context.

And reflection gives you all three.

It helps you:

- Spot recurring mistakes so you can preempt them.

- Identify your own tendencies under pressure.

- Track your evolving values, priorities, and blind spots.

- Reinforce the mental models that actually worked.

It also helps you notice internal shifts: where your fear subsided, where your courage grew, where your thinking deepened. Those aren't visible in performance reviews. But they're real. And they matter.

Building a Reflective Practice Without Turning Into a Journaling Guru

You don't need to light a candle and write poetry about your decision cycles. You just need a system. One that fits your brain, your schedule, and your attention span.

Try one of these:

1. The 3W Reflection

At the end of a day, week, or project, ask:

- What went well?

- What didn't?

- What will I do differently next time?

Keep it short. 5 minutes. Bullet points. That's it. Do it consistently and you'll be stunned how much you learn.

2. Wins + Gaps Tracker

Keep a split-page tracker with two columns:

- Wins – where you handled something well (and why it worked)

- Gaps – where something faltered (and what you missed)

This helps you avoid only tracking mistakes (which fuels imposter syndrome) or only celebrating wins (which creates blind spots). You need both. Side by side.

3. Weekly Debrief with a Peer

Find a thought partner and set a 30-minute weekly chat. Focus on process, not venting. What decision did you make? What challenged you? What did you learn?

Bonus: You'll sharpen each other's thinking and build shared language for solving problems.

Making Reflection Actionable

The biggest risk with reflection is that it stays passive. A mental scrapbook. Something you understand but never use.

To prevent that, close every reflection loop with one of these:

- A decision you'll make differently next time

- A habit you'll test for the next 7 days

- A blind spot you'll ask someone to help you watch for

Reflection without action is therapy. Reflection with action is evolution.

What Happens When You Don't Reflect

You repeat things. You solve the same types of problems, with the same types of errors, wondering why nothing ever sticks. You keep feeling "busy" but not better. And worst of all, you miss the bigger story of your own growth.

Because reflection isn't just about fixing mistakes. It's about capturing progress. Without it, you might not realize how far you've come.

You forget that a year ago, you were scared to make that call. That six months ago, you wouldn't have caught that flaw in the plan. That last week, you said something in a meeting that used to terrify you.

Reflection replays the film. It reminds you that growth is happening, just not always where you were looking.

Final Thought: Reflection Is a Mirror, Not a Scorecard

You're not collecting gold stars. You're collecting clarity.

So take the time. Close the loop. Study yourself like a system you actually care about. Because if you don't learn from your patterns, you'll live in them. Over and over.

And the most effective thinkers, the ones who sustain, not just spike, aren't the fastest. They're the most aware.

They don't just solve problems. They solve themselves.

Keeping the Game Alive

Now that you're equipped to make smarter decisions, solve complex problems, and tackle challenges with confidence, it's your turn to keep the momentum going.

By sharing your honest thoughts about *Think Sharp: How Anyone Can Master Critical Thinking and Problem-Solving for Smarter Decisions and Career Success* on Amazon, you can guide other curious minds toward the tools they need to thrive.

Why Your Review Matters

Your voice helps others: career climbers, lifelong learners, and ambitious problem-solvers discover the insights they're searching for. Your review isn't just feedback; it's a way to pass on the spark of inspiration and ensure critical thinking continues to empower people everywhere.

Thank you for your help. The art of critical thinking thrives when we share what we've learned, and you're playing a vital role in that journey.

Ready to make a difference?

Click here to leave your review on Amazon. https://www.amazon.com/review/review-your-purchases/?asin=B0F35WJHD8

Thank you for being part of this journey. Let's keep the game alive!

Warm regards,

Renae C. Linde

STAYING SHARP

Y ou made it.

Not just to the end of a book, but through a mental reset that most people never commit to. You've sifted through decision traps, cracked open old biases, rewired how you think under pressure, and sharpened your ability to speak and solve with clarity. That's not light reading. It's not entertainment. It's work, quiet, cognitive work with very real emotional cost. And if you've done the exercises, if you've run these tools through your actual life instead of just nodding at them, then this isn't the end at all. It's the inflection point.

You now have something most people never build: a system for making sense of chaos.

And that matters, because the world doesn't get easier from here. Information isn't slowing down. Problems aren't getting simpler. People aren't becoming less reactive. If anything, we're all more tired, more distracted, more flooded with noise. The ability to stop and say, *"Wait. Let's break this down,"* is no longer optional. It's your edge.

But let's pause for a minute before you go charging back into your inbox with a new framework. Because this isn't about "maximizing productivity" or chasing another badge of intellectual achievement. It's about something quieter. It's about being able to trust your own thinking, even when things go sideways. Especially then.

That kind of trust doesn't come from a single read-through. It's built through practice. Through reflection. Through failure. Through the moment you freeze mid-conversation, forget everything in this book, say the wrong thing, then go back and analyze what happened, not to self-punish, but to understand. That's where real mastery takes hold: in the clarity to see what went wrong and the ability to repair it.

So no, this book doesn't end with a list of "power affirmations" or a pat on the back. It ends with a challenge: Start treating your mind the way athletes treat their bodies. You don't get strong by understanding pushups. You get strong by doing them, consistently, with resistance. That's how critical thinking works, too. It's not a personality trait. It's a form of disciplined repetition.

Let's ground that challenge in something real. Take a moment and think about the last high-stakes decision you made, professionally or personally. What went right? What went wrong? What assumptions did you make without realizing it? What emotions were driving your logic, whether you admitted them or not?

Now take that decision and walk it back through the tools you've learned:

- What information did you filter out, and was that filtering useful or biased?

- What mental shortcuts (heuristics) were you relying on?

- Did you pause to question your initial framing of the problem?

- Did you seek out disconfirming evidence, or just gather proof for what you already believed?

- Did you consider how your communication style might have shaped others' responses?

- Were you solving for the surface issue or the deeper pattern underneath?

This isn't theoretical. These are real diagnostic questions. They aren't meant to make you overthink every move. They're meant to give you clarity when it counts. When time is short. When emotions run high. When stakes are personal. You're not trying to become a robot. You're trying to stop being yanked around by every mental shortcut your brain throws at you. That takes awareness. It takes humility. And it takes a different relationship with your own mind, less reactive, more reflective.

Let's be honest. You're going to forget some of this. That's fine. Forgetting is part of the cycle. The goal isn't perfect retention. The goal is to make forgetting less costly. To recover faster. To notice the warning signs earlier. And to shorten the distance between making a mistake and learning from it.

That's the real payoff of critical thinking: agility. Not rigidity. Not always having the "right" answer, but being able to course-correct faster than most people even realize something's off. It's being the one in the room who can see past the noise without needing to control everything. It's knowing when to pause, when to speak, and when to pivot.

And yes, it's also knowing when to let something go.

Because not every problem is yours to solve. Not every argument is worth dissecting. Not every flawed idea is your job to correct. Part of thinking sharply is learning to choose your battles, and that includes walking away from circular debates, unproductive meetings, and people who want attention more than solutions.

That's not defeat. That's discernment.

Let's talk about power, not the kind you flex over others, but the kind that stabilizes you under pressure. The kind that lets you walk into a heated conversation, a high-stakes meeting, or a personal crisis and not immediately lose your internal compass. That power doesn't come from always being the smartest person in the room. It comes from knowing how to think when your ego wants to react. It's in the pause before the response. The breath before the opinion. The space you build between stimulus and action.

You've trained for that. Quietly, consistently, through every chapter.

You've learned to identify your own blind spots. To recognize when a decision is being hijacked by fear of failure or the illusion of certainty. You've learned to untangle emotion from logic without denying either one. You've built tools to clarify your thinking when things get messy, and to communicate with precision instead of spiraling into defensiveness. That's not just cognitive skill. That's resilience.

And here's the thing: most people never build it. They might consume information constantly. They might be great at multitasking or winging it in meetings. But that's not the same as mental clarity. That's not the same as knowing how to untangle a tough decision or decode a misaligned conversation or see when the solution you're chasing is still rooted in a flawed assumption.

Clarity is rare because it requires discipline.

And discipline is uncomfortable. It's slower than instinct. It forces you to ask hard questions when shortcuts would feel so much better. It doesn't guarantee a smooth ride. But it does give you a set of rails to run on, especially when emotion and urgency threaten to derail your logic.

So here's what I want you to do with everything you've learned: make it personal.

Go back through the chapters, yes, literally. Pick one exercise that made you pause. One tool that hit a nerve. Maybe it was the bias you didn't realize you held. Maybe it was a moment where your communication style caused more confusion than clarity. Maybe it was the realization that you've been solving the wrong problems because the framing was off from the start.

Revisit that. Go deeper. Apply it again, this time with fresh eyes. Because the first read-through is just that: exposure. The second time? That's where you train. That's where insight becomes instinct.

If you're still in the early stages of building your critical thinking practice, here's a short list of real-world starting points, low-cost, high-impact places to apply what you've learned:

- Review the last three emails you sent. Did you write them for clarity or for control? Did you state your position or signal your anxiety?

- Think through a recent disagreement. What were you actually arguing about, facts, values, priorities, or interpretations?

- Pick a recurring frustration. Is it a logistics issue? A communication gap? A misaligned goal? Or a decision paralysis disguised as busyness?

- Audit your information intake. Are you actively curating what you consume, or passively drowning in it? Do you know the difference between being informed and being overwhelmed?

- Choose a habit loop you want to break. Don't start with discipline. Start with better framing. What problem is that habit solving? What's the payoff? What's the hidden cost?

These are not dramatic overhauls. They're micro-movements. But the compound interest is real.

Because you can read a hundred books on decision-making, but if you're still reacting from fear, bias, urgency, or pride, then you're not thinking, you're just surviving. Thinking happens in the space between your trigger and your choice. And building that space, moment by moment, is what gives you back your agency.

This doesn't mean you become perfect. Or emotionless. It means you become aware.

And once you're aware, you have leverage. You can adjust. You can lead conversations instead of being dragged by them. You can notice when your own reasoning is breaking down, before it costs you the outcome you want. You can stay anchored, even when others around you are flailing.

That's not just a personal advantage. That's a leadership skill.

Not the performative kind, where you posture on a stage or craft the perfect LinkedIn post. I mean the kind of leadership that happens in real rooms with real people under real pressure. The kind that steadies a team. That clears a path. That makes hard decisions without scapegoating, spiraling, or shutting down.

And that kind of leadership, personal or professional, starts with internal clarity.

Not confidence. Not charisma. Not charm.

Clarity.

Let's strip away the motivational language and face this directly: most people don't want to think. They want relief. Certainty. A path with guardrails so they don't have to question every step. And that's human. Questioning is work. Doubt is exhausting. But so is regret. So is wasting a decade on the wrong strategy because no one paused to ask the harder questions.

You're not here to avoid discomfort. You're here to build tolerance for it.

That's the paradox of sharp thinking: it makes your life clearer, not easier. You'll see sooner when someone's manipulating a conversation. You'll catch your own cognitive distortions before they snowball. You'll start noticing when a decision doesn't need more input, it needs you to stop rationalizing and move. But all of that clarity comes with cost: responsibility. Because once you see the pattern, you can't unsee it. Once you understand the mechanics, you can't pretend it's fate.

And that's where growth lives, not in knowing more, but in acting differently.

Let's say that again for the achiever in your head who thinks more input is always the solution: growth is not about knowing more. It's about changing what you do with what you already know. That includes pausing before you escalate. Clarifying what you're solving before you solve it. Asking yourself, *"What's the real goal here?"* before diving into strategy mode.

Too often we treat thinking as an academic exercise, something separate from who we are in conflict or decision. But every fight, every meeting, every internal tug-of-war is a thinking moment. And your job isn't to perfect the outcome. It's to engage with that moment more skillfully than you did last time. That's it.

Because let's be honest, skillful thinking won't make you invincible. It won't keep you from overreacting, or saying something you regret, or choosing a wrong path. What it will do is help you shorten the recovery time. It will help you say, *"Ah. There it is. That's what I missed. That's where I rushed. That's the pattern I keep repeating."* And instead of spiraling into shame or doubling down on bad logic, you'll do something smarter: you'll pivot.

That's mastery.

Not perfection. Not rigid discipline. Just a smarter next move, made sooner.

And the longer you train that pivot, the more natural it becomes. Eventually, you'll start to recognize your default reactions not as data. A cue. An invitation to shift. That's the quiet transformation of critical thinking, understanding yourself differently inside it.

Because every time you catch your own flawed assumption, you get a little more honest. Every time you slow down before delivering a snap judgment, you gain a little more control. Every time you ask a better question instead of rehearsing your next rebuttal, you build trust, within yourself, and with others.

That's not just a cognitive upgrade. That's a relational one.

And yes, it's deeply emotional.

If no one has told you this yet, let me: the clearer your thinking becomes, the lonelier some spaces will feel. You'll stop falling for surface-level charisma. You'll opt out of groupthink. You'll be the one who says, *"Let's slow down"* when everyone else is chasing momentum. You'll be misunderstood sometimes, not because you're arrogant, but because clarity has a frequency that not everyone's ready to hear.

Don't let that push you back into mental clutter just to stay connected. Don't water down your process for comfort. Let your thinking be a filter. Let it draw in the kind of collaboration, leadership, and decision-making that doesn't run on panic or politeness.

Let it make you sharper, yes, but also steadier. More grounded. Less afraid to pause.

There's no trophy for that. But there is peace.

And in a world that profits off your distraction, peace is a kind of rebellion.

So where do you go from here?

You go forward, intentionally. Not with a checklist, not with a five-year plan, but with a habit: pause, reflect, apply. That's it. That's the core loop. Pause before defaulting. Reflect before reacting. Apply what you've trained, because you value your time, your energy, and your relationships too much to waste them on lazy thinking.

The people who get ahead, and stay sane, aren't always the ones with the most talent or the most knowledge. They're the ones who've built mental flexibility. The ones who can separate noise from relevance. The ones who don't get swept up in urgency theater or ego battles. The ones who stay curious when everyone else is scrambling for certainty.

You don't need to be brilliant. You need to be clear.

And clarity isn't some elite intellectual trait. It's built by consistently doing the things most people avoid: slowing down when they want to rush, asking questions when they'd rather assume, and changing their mind when new evidence demands it. That's rare. But it's trainable. And now, you know how to train it.

Here's what I'd suggest next, not as an assignment, but as a way to stay sharp when the initial motivation fades:

- Pick one chapter a month to revisit. Re-read. Apply one exercise in real time. Watch how it shifts your choices or conversations. Then document the results.

- Track your decision-making. Not obsessively, but enough to build pattern recognition. Write down one high-stakes decision a week. Later, review the outcome and what thinking style you used.

- Practice talking through your thinking. In meetings, in conflict, with mentors, start naming your process. Say things like, *"Here's how I arrived at this,"* or *"I'm noticing a bias here."* The more you do this, the more influence you gain, not just by sounding smart, but by modeling clarity for others.

- Teach someone else. The fastest way to internalize a skill is to share it. Whether it's a teammate, a friend, or your kid, pass it on. Not the whole book. Just one insight that helped you. Make it practical. Make it human.

None of these are flashy. They don't look good on LinkedIn. But over time, they build something rare: cognitive maturity. That's what people feel when they talk to someone who listens well, asks real questions, and doesn't flinch in uncertainty. You can't fake that. You can't rush it. But you can build it.

And here's a quiet truth most people miss: sharp thinking doesn't always look like confidence. Sometimes it looks like listening longer than expected. Sometimes it looks like saying *"I don't know"* without flinching. Sometimes it looks like asking a simple, disarming question that no one else thought to ask because they were too busy trying to look smart.

You don't need to win every argument. You don't need to solve every problem. You just need to bring better thinking to the moments that matter.

The rest follows.

So take what works. Leave what doesn't. Come back when life throws a curveball or your brain starts to slip into autopilot. This isn't a one-and-done read. It's a toolset. A way of seeing. And now, it's yours.

Use it well.

Pause. Reflect. Apply.

Then teach someone else how to do the same.

That's how this spreads.

That's how we change the game.

More from Renae C. Linde

Money Smarts

A Practical Guide to Financial Independence for Young Adults

An introduction to the real-world financial concepts every young adult should know: income, expenses, saving, credit, and investing. A practical guide to navigating money choices with confidence in daily life.

Ethical Hustle

Making a Living Without Selling Your Soul

For anyone tempted by hustle culture or quick-win schemes, this book shows how to build a career and income that reflect both ambition and integrity, success you won't regret later.

Toxic No More

Proven Strategies to Overcome Destructive Patterns

and Build Emotional Intelligence for Strong,

Healthy Relationships

Clear thinking also requires clear relationships. This guide helps you recognize destructive patterns, build emotional intelligence, and strengthen the way you communicate at work and at home.

The Great Divide: Americas Political Tug-of-War

Why Were so Divided and What We Can Do About It

An accessible look at how polarization shapes the way we think and argue. It offers insight and tools for making sense of public debate without losing clarity or your cool.

References

Allen, D. (2001). Getting things done: The art of stress-free productivity. Penguin.

Boyd, J. (1987). A discourse on winning and losing. Air University Library. [Unpublished briefing slides; foundational source of the OODA loop.]

Brown, B. (2018). *Dare to lead: Brave work. Tough conversations. Whole hearts.* Random House.

Caruso, D. R., & Salovey, P. (2004). *The emotionally intelligent manager: How to develop and use the four key emotional skills of leadership.* Jossey-Bass.

Colzato, L. S., Ozturk, A., & Hommel, B. (2012). Meditate to create: The impact of focused-attention and open-monitoring training on convergent and divergent thinking. Frontiers in Psychology, 3, 116. https://doi.org/10.3389/fpsyg.2012.00116

De Bono, E. (1985). Six thinking hats. Little, Brown and Company.

De Bono, E. (1992). Serious creativity: Using the power of lateral thinking to create new ideas. HarperBusiness.

Dweck, C. S. (2006). Mindset: The new psychology of success. Random House.

Edmonson, A. (2019). *The fearless organization: Creating psychological safety in the workplace for learning, innovation, and growth.* Wiley.

Forte, T. (2022). Building a second brain: A proven method to organize your digital life and unlock your creative potential. Atria Books.

Goleman, D. (1995). *Emotional intelligence: Why it can matter more than IQ.* Bantam Books.

Goleman, D. (2006). *Social intelligence: The new science of human relationships.* Bantam Books.

Grant, A. (2021). *Think again: The power of knowing what you don't know.* Viking.

Heath, C., & Heath, D. (2007). Made to stick: Why some ideas survive and others die. Random House.

Heath, C., & Heath, D. (2013). Decisive: How to make better choices in life and work. Crown Business.

Kahneman, D. (2011). *Thinking, fast and slow.* Farrar, Straus and Giroux.

Klein, G. (1999). Sources of power: How people make decisions. MIT Press.

Lencioni, P. (2002). *The five dysfunctions of a team: A leadership fable.* Jossey-Bass.

Leroy, S. (2009). Why is it so hard to do my work? The challenge of attention residue when switching between work tasks. Organizational Behavior and Human Decision Processes, 109(2), 168–181. https://doi.org/10.1016/j.obhdp.2009.04.002

Rock, D. (2009). *Your brain at work: Strategies for overcoming distraction, regaining focus, and working smarter all day long.* HarperBusiness.

Serrat, O. (2017). The SCAMPER technique. In Knowledge Solutions (pp. 833–838). Springer. https://doi.org/10.1007/978-9 81-10-0983-9_92

Sterman, J. D. (2000). Business dynamics: Systems thinking and modeling for a complex world. Irwin/McGraw-Hill.

Stone, D., Patton, B., & Heen, S. (2010). *Difficult conversations: How to discuss what matters most* (2nd ed.). Penguin Books.

Sweller, J. (2011). Cognitive load theory. Psychology of Learning and Motivation, 55, 37–76. https://doi.org/10.1016/B978-0-12 -387691-1.00002-8

Tracy, B. (2001). Eat that frog!: 21 great ways to stop procrastinating and get more done in less time. Berrett-Koehler Publishers.

Zeidan, F., Johnson, S. K., Diamond, B. J., David, Z., & Goolkasian, P. (2010). Mindfulness meditation improves cognition: Evidence of brief mental training. Consciousness and Cognition, 19(2), 597–605. https://doi.org/10.1016/j.concog.2010.03.014